"Edward Hahnenberg brings the best insights from his recent works on ministry and vocation into a resource that is accessible and delightful to read. Weaving personal stories, references to pop culture, classical questions, history, and a good introduction to Catholic theology, this work is an invitation to think about ministry in light of the core convictions of our faith. No better place to ground the discernment of the vocation to Christian service than in the contemplation of the mysteries of the Triune God, Jesus, the Spirit, and the Church! *Theology for Ministry* is an excellent guide for such discernment."

— Hosffman Ospino
Boston College School of Theology and Ministry

"This volume is the fruit of a gifted theologian's deep reflection on the lived life of the Church, in particular, lay ministry, in light of our theological tradition. The preposition *for* in the title is central: this work is at the service of lay ministers, inviting deep reflection on 'their own' experience, and the theology which grounds it more deeply. Discussion questions encourage a pondering of experience, as well as the themes of vocation, God, Jesus Christ, the Spirit, the Church and ministry, each presented with great lucidity. Many sources inform Hahnenberg's work, including varied ecclesial documents, spiritual writers, theologians old and new, contemporary artists, but most especially stories of lay ministers (and his own stories) of the wellsprings of their faith and commitment to service. This is a rich resource for spiritual growth, and for a deepening of identity as lay ministers."

— Zeni Fox
Professor of Pastoral Theology
Seton Hall University

"In chapter 4, Hahnenberg says he has the gift of explaining things— to which I say 'Amen!' This book simply explains why we do what we do. The chapter titles: *Called . . . By God . . . Through Christ . . . In the Spirit . . . With Others . . . For Others* provide a framework and a context in history, theology, and community for ministry. The reflection questions in each chapter anchor his themes in the reader's lived experiences, making this a valuable resource for formal and informal formation programs and for varied ministry settings."

— Robert J. McCarty, DMin
Executive Director
National Federation for Catholic Youth Ministry

Theology for Ministry

An Introduction for Lay Ministers

Edward P. Hahnenberg

LITURGICAL PRESS
Collegeville, Minnesota

www.litpress.org

1	2	3	4	5	6	7	8	9

Library of Congress Cataloging-in-Publication Data

Hahnenberg, Edward P.
   Theology for ministry : an introduction for lay ministers /
by Edward P. Hahnenberg.
     pages   cm
   Includes bibliographical references.
   ISBN 978-0-8146-3521-6 — ISBN 978-0-8146-3546-9 (ebook)
    1. Catholic Church—Doctrines.   2. Lay ministry—Catholic Church.
3. Laity—Catholic Church.   I. Title.

  BX1753.H225   2014
  262'.152—dc23   2013045662

"Be transformed by the renewal of your mind."

—Romans 12:2

Contents

Preface

God is at work in your life.

The fact that you are holding this book in your hands is a sign that you *know* God is at work—and that you want to respond.

For many Christians, this recognition leads to a deepening of faith. For some, it prompts a desire to serve. It awakens a call to ministry.

Since the Second Vatican Council (1962–65), Catholics have come to the realization that the mission of the church belongs to *everyone*—clergy and laity alike. One of the clearest signs of this new awareness is the growth of various forms of lay ministry over the past fifty years. Tens of thousands have stepped up to serve. They are women and men, volunteers and full-time professionals, people working in parishes and out in the community. Their ministries range from education and liturgy to chaplaincy, administration, and advocacy. Virtually no area of Catholic life today has not been touched by the presence of generous and committed lay ministers.

You are a part of this story.

You also have your own story to tell.

This book is an opportunity to reflect on your story—to reflect on your own call to serve—and to place that call within the context of the church and its two-thousand-year-old tradition. The following pages invite you to think about your experience in light of your faith. They offer an introduction to theology.

An Introduction . . .

Theology for Ministry is written for laypeople interested or involved in ministry who have little or no theological background.

If you are a volunteer hungry to learn more about your faith, a student just beginning a ministry program, or a seasoned lay ecclesial minister looking for a deeper grounding for your work, these pages offer a basic introduction to several important areas of Catholic theology—always with an eye to what it means for ministry. Given its broad definition of ministry, this book could also serve the needs of parish discussion groups, small faith communities, retreat teams, lay leaders within Catholic institutions, high school and elementary school teachers, young adults preparing for service programs, and anyone interested in knowing more about his or her faith and finding ways to serve more fully the mission of Christ.

Ministry, as I take it, is any activity done on behalf of the church community that proclaims, celebrates, and serves the reign of God. This little definition raises some big questions. Who is God? What did Jesus mean by the reign of God? How do we understand the church? Whose activity are we talking about and what do they do? As soon as we start thinking about our ministry, we become theologians. We begin to explore the major themes of our faith.

The following chapters introduce six of these themes: the notion of vocation, the doctrine of God, Jesus Christ, the Holy Spirit, church, and ministry. Each chapter begins by inviting reflection on one's personal experience, then surveys the history and church teaching on the topic, and ends by exploring the implications of all of this for the work of ministry.

. . . To Theology

The decision to start each chapter by reflecting on experience flows out of the very nature of the theological task. The word *theology* literally means "the study of God." But that definition is not so helpful. How can we study God? We cannot invite God to sit down for an interview. We cannot bring God into a lab or put God under a microscope. God is the infinite mystery who always eludes our grasp, transcending all our powers of comprehension. We cannot study this mystery. The best we can do is study *the human experience* of this mystery.[1]

Therefore, a more helpful definition may be one that goes back over nine hundred years to the medieval bishop St. Anselm of Canterbury: theology is "faith seeking understanding."

We start with the human experience of faith. And then we try our best to understand it. Faith is not just a set of beliefs or a kind of blind trust. According to the Bible, the belief and trust associated with faith flow out of something far more fundamental: a personal encounter with God. At its heart, faith is an encounter—an *experience* of divine mystery.

This mystery permeates our lives. We catch a glimpse of it whenever we awaken to a moment of genuine clarity, or feel in our bones the absolute goodness of life, or hold out hope in the face of despair, or sense some deeper meaning and purpose behind our daily routine. Encounters with God are not limited to a burning bush or a voice from heaven. Anyone who has ever experienced "something more" to life has already brushed up against the divine mystery. Theology is simply the attempt to make sense of these experiences of "something more." We almost can't help but do theology! When we feel God at work in our lives, we want to know more. Faith (the encounter with divine mystery) seeks understanding.

Reflecting on the encounter with divine mystery is a profoundly personal activity. But it always takes place in a larger communal context. The Catholic tradition has long held that we can learn a lot by bringing our individual experiences into dialogue with the experiences of others. The church is a place for that to happen. Through the church community, we engage not only those who are alive today, but also those who lived centuries ago. We join in on a lively conversation that has been going on for more than two thousand years.

The following pages hope to continue this conversation. We bring together the past and the present by encouraging a dialogue between our *religious tradition*, on the one hand, and our *contemporary lives*, on the other.

Theology done in the academy today is marked by a variety of different methods. The approach of this book is simple: We lift up what the tradition has taught and hold it alongside what we have experienced ourselves. And we ask how the two illuminate one another.

Insight emerges from this back and forth dialogue between tradition and experience, between past and present, between doctrine and life. Sometimes this dialogue leads to a deepening of what we already believe. Sometimes it leads to a whole new way of thinking. Often ancient ideas become surprisingly relevant. We start to notice things about our lives we never noticed before. We learn to pay better attention. We come to see how God is at work.

Acknowledgements

I owe the overall framework for this book to Part One of the *Catechism of the Catholic Church* and its more readable companion, the *United States Catholic Catechism for Adults*. Both of these texts lay out basic Catholic beliefs according to the order of the Creed. First comes the experience of faith ("I believe . . ."), followed by God, Jesus Christ, the Holy Spirit, the church, and its mission. Thus the following chapters place our call to serve within the same pattern. We are: (1) Called . . . (2) By God . . . (3) Through Christ . . . (4) In the Spirit . . . (5) With Others . . . (6) For Others.

Each chapter includes recommended reading. There you can find references to the catechism sections that correspond to the material covered in the chapter. (A quick internet search will take you to the websites of the Vatican and the United States Conference of Catholic Bishops, which contain access to these texts, as well as other resources.) The recommended reading also includes additional titles for those readers who would like to go deeper. Rather than catalogue classic works or suggest heavy volumes, I list short, accessible works of theology—books that I think would serve well as a "next step" for exploring the ideas introduced here.

As I look over these ideas, and think about the chapters that follow, I am painfully aware of how much I have left out, of how much my own experiences limit what I am able to see and what I am able to say. I hope you can take these shortcomings as an invitation. Fill in your own experiences. Ask your own questions. Add your own insights. You really don't need much to get started doing theology—just an openness to mystery and to your own graced experience.

My own experience has been graced by many people who have helped bring this project to completion. I thank, first and foremost, my family—my wife, Julie, and our three girls, Kate, Meg, and Abby—who remind me every day just how much God is at work in my life.

I am grateful for the support and encouragement that comes from my colleagues at John Carroll University, particularly for the concrete assistance offered so generously by Kathy Merhar and my graduate assistant Meagen Howe. Thanks too to the whole team at Liturgical Press, especially Hans Christoffersen, Barry Hudock, and Andy Edwards.

As many of the stories below suggest, I have learned a lot from my students. And I thank them. In a special way I want to thank the many lay ministers I have come to know over the years. Early in my career, my academic work called me out into parishes, ministry associations, and dioceses across the country. There I met a community of incredible people—faithful disciples and dedicated, gifted ministers. These lay women and men became my teachers, my mentors, and often my friends. Their commitment, hope, and good humor remain an inspiration. As a small sign of gratitude, I dedicate this book to them.

1

Called . . .

In the sixth month, the angel Gabriel was sent from God to a town of Galilee called Nazareth, to a virgin betrothed to a man named Joseph, of the house of David, and the virgin's name was Mary. And coming to her, he said, "Hail, favored one! The Lord is with you." But she was greatly troubled at what was said and pondered what sort of greeting this might be. Then the angel said to her, "Do not be afraid, Mary, for you have found favor with God. Behold, you will conceive in your womb and bear a son, and you shall name him Jesus." (Luke 1:26-31)

God called Mary. And in that call were all the features of a genuine vocation. The call came from God. It deepened a relationship. It led to transformation. It gave a mission. This pattern of call can be found again and again in the Bible. It extends over the course of Christian history. And it continues in our own lives.

When Mary heard the angel's words, she was startled. She doubted. How can this be? It's impossible. When Gabriel reminded her that "nothing is impossible for God," Mary accepted. She said *yes* to God's call. "May it be done to me according to your word" (Luke 1:38).

With that *yes*, Christ came into the world.

Starting with Experience

In the middle of class a few years ago, one of my students, Christine, shared the story of how she got into ministry.

1

Christine had been a successful corporate trainer. She loved what she did, and she was paid well to do it. But in the midst of it all, something was missing.

Christine said she would get angry with God. Why couldn't she just be happy? Things were going great. Why wasn't she satisfied? She would lie in bed at night arguing with God, shouting up at the ceiling, "What, God? What? What do you want?"

She gradually came to a realization, "I knew in my heart I had to help others."

So Christine took a terrifying leap of faith: She quit her job and entered a ministry program. When I met her, Christine had already been working for several years as a chaplain in a state prison for men.

After class that night, I thought about Christine. I thought about the way she said *yes* to God's invitation. And it occurred to me that her story was not so different from Mary's story. Just like Mary, when Christine said *yes* to her call, Christ came into the world.

Every *yes* to God's call is an incarnation of Jesus Christ. He "takes on flesh" (*in carne*) in our lives of love and service to others. Christine would often share stories of the men she knew in prison—men who are invisible to the rest of us, forgotten by our society, locked out of sight. Christine was there with them, listening to their problems, challenging their stubbornness, caring for their needs. She was Christ to them. She was awakening Christ *in* them.

That night I wrote in my journal, "Christ enters the world again and again!"

After Christine shared her story, the other members of the class thanked her. One student started to worry out loud that he had never felt such a clear call, or made such a radical decision. He said he had no idea what God's plan was for his life.

Another student responded that she didn't like the idea of "God's plan." It felt too fixed, too final. She said God's call is not like a detailed roadmap with the whole journey laid out in advance. It's more like GPS, she said. When we get lost, God is right there to get us back on track, "Recalculating . . . Recalculating . . ."

We all laughed.

In the end, we concluded that every call is unique. As Christine put it, "If you're not up at three in the morning talking to the ceiling, then God is probably not calling you to a radical change!"

Christine's insight encourages us to turn from her story to our own.

How have you heard the call to serve?

Why are you reading this book? Why are you engaged in ministry? Why are you thinking about theology?

What got you on the path that you are on? What events led you to where you are now? The story of your call to serve is as unique as you are. Did God's call come as an invitation out of the blue? Or did it come through the constant encouragement of a friend? Was it a sudden life change? Or years of volunteering that led, step-by-step, to greater and greater involvement? Is God stirring you in prayer? Is something missing at work? Do you see a need that no one else is addressing? Are you finally acknowledging a gift that, until now, you have been too shy to share?

> *Pause and reflect on your own experience. How would you tell your "vocation story"? If it helps, write it down. Prepare a two- or three-page narrative that begins, "I first felt the call to serve. . . ." Name the people who mentored you along. Describe the places that shaped your decisions. Explain the events that stand out. Share the emotions that you felt.*

Revelation

This chapter offers an introduction to a theology of vocation. Here we take vocation, or "calling," in a broad and inclusive sense. God calls every single one of us. And God calls us in a variety of ways. *Vocation* can refer to one's ministry. It can also mean one's state of life. It can also describe the more general call to discipleship—what the Second Vatican Council termed "the universal vocation to holiness." Our vocations are multiple, interrelated, and overlapping. They include lifelong decisions and more modest commitments. They evolve. They change. But what every vocation shares is a sense of meaning that comes when we live our lives as a response to God's invitation.

The idea that God *calls* us raises the question of how God *communicates* with us. Thus before talking about vocation, we have to say something about one of the most fundamental concepts of theology: Revelation.

The word *revelation* means "to remove the veil." It refers to God's act of disclosing God's self to humanity—an act that lifts the veil between us and the divine.

For a long time, Catholic theologians assumed revelation was all about *words*. Revelation seemed to be a process by which God transmitted to us a long list of facts—interesting information that God thought we ought to know: the Trinity is three persons in one nature, Jesus is fully human and fully divine, there are seven sacraments, and so on. In such a scheme, *faith* was simply the act of intellectual assent. It was accepting these facts without any evidence. Because this approach reduced revelation to statements, or propositions, it could be called a propositional theology of revelation.

We see an example of this approach in a funny scene near the beginning of Mel Brooks' irreverent film *History of the World: Part I*. In the scene, Brooks comes down from a mountain dressed like Moses, wearing a long robe and white beard. He is carrying three stone tablets.

Brooks looks out on the crowd and, in all biblical seriousness, proclaims: "Hear me, O hear me. . . . The Lord, the Lord Jehovah has given unto you these fifteen—"

At that moment, one of the tablets slips from his arms and shatters into pieces on the ground. Brooks looks down, looks up, and without missing a beat, continues: "*Ten* . . . given these *Ten* Commandments for all to obey!"

There is a lot that is silly in this scene. But at root, its humor lies in its theology. The joke works because it relies on a propositional theology of revelation. It presumes that revelation is secret information from God. We laugh at the joke (or we groan!) because we wonder what words were lost in that shattered third tablet.

Recent church teaching has not denied the importance of words, but it has placed these words in a broader context. God is not primarily interested in sharing information, God is interested in sharing *God's very self*. Revelation is first and foremost God's offer of friendship. It is about a relationship. Faith is our response. It is trusting our whole selves to this friendship. Words are important, but only insofar as they help us name and deepen our relationship with God.

The Second Vatican Council affirmed this more relational approach when it taught: "By this revelation, then, the invisible God, from the fullness of his love, addresses men and women as his friends, and lives among them, in order to invite and receive them into his own company" (*Dei Verbum* 2).[1] God wants to be our friend, and so creates us and comes to us. That simple insight is the heart of the Catholic theology of revelation.

The distinction between propositional and relational approaches offers a clue to a proper understanding of vocation. In discerning our vocation, we should not be looking for a lot of words—clear instructions from God. Instead we should be opening ourselves to a relationship. We should be looking for the ways in which God loves us and looking for ways to love back. To discover our unique way of loving God and loving others is to discover our vocation.

The Bible: The Story of God's Call

With the words "Let there be light," God called the world into existence. God called Adam and Eve to dwell in the Garden of Eden. God called Abraham and Sarah to leave their homeland and journey toward an unknown future. God called Moses to lead the people of Israel out of Egypt and into the Promised Land. As Israel became a great nation, God called kings and prophets to guide the people. When the time came, God called

Mary and Joseph and John the Baptist to prepare the way for the Messiah. Through his life, death, and resurrection, Jesus extended God's call to the whole world. From beginning to end, the Bible is a story of call.

A propositional approach to revelation can lead to a literal approach to the Bible, which Catholicism tries to avoid. God did not pick up the phone and dictate the words of scripture to its authors. Rather, God invited the people Israel into a relationship. The people responded. And the Bible tells that story. But it does so through a variety of narratives, written over the course of a thousand years, by many different authors, in many different genres and styles.

In the Old Testament, for example, we find three broad types of writings: *historical books*, which describe God's interactions with Israel (these include, among others, the first five books of the Bible, known as the Pentateuch); *prophetic books*, which recount the prophets' warnings against sin (Isaiah, Jeremiah, Ezekiel, and more); and *wisdom books*, which offer prayers and reflections on life (the most well-known is the book of Psalms). The New Testament is also made up of different kinds of literature, including: *the four gospels* (stories of Jesus' life); *the Acts of the Apostles* (a history of the early church); and *the epistles* (a series of letters written by St. Paul and other early Christians).

The Old Testament

In the book of Genesis, God extends an improbable invitation to Abraham and his wife Sarah. In their story, we discover the basic features of the biblical notion of vocation.

First of all, God selected Abram from among all people not because of anything Abram had done. God's call came out of God's pure generosity and love. The initiative was God's alone. "No longer will you be called Abram; your name will be Abraham, for I am making you the father of a multitude of nations" (Gen 17:5).

Second, Abraham was called to a relationship. God desired a lasting bond—a covenant—with Abraham and his family. God also pledged to remain close: I will be your God, and you will be my people. This relationship was transformative—a third feature of the biblical call. When Abraham was told that he would become the father of a great nation, with more descendants than the stars in the sky, he burst out laughing. When his wife Sarah later heard the news, she laughed too. "We are too old to start anything new," seemed to be their shared sentiment. But the grace of God's invitation opened them up to new life. They were transformed by God's trust in them.

Finally, God's call implies a mission. Like all authentic vocations, Abraham's call extended outward. It drew him into God's saving purpose. Abraham was called not for himself, but so that, through him "all the families of the earth will find blessing" (Gen 12:3).

As the Bible stories continue, the descendants of Abraham and Sarah multiply. These descendants migrated to Egypt and were eventually enslaved. When God called Moses to lead the Israelites out of Egypt, Moses resisted. He stalled and searched for an excuse: "Who am I that I should go to Pharaoh? . . . What if they will not believe me? . . . I have never been eloquent . . . Please, Lord, send someone else!" But God saw in Moses something Moses did not see in himself. God sent him ahead with the promise that he would not be alone: "I will assist you in speaking and teach you what you are to say" (Exod 4:12).

After Moses led Israel across the Red Sea, on to Mount Sinai, and through forty years of wandering in the desert, the people of God finally entered into the Promised Land. God called first Saul, and then David to serve as king. Israel became a great nation, fulfilling God's promise to Abraham long ago. But Israel did not always live up to its vocation. When Israel failed in its faithfulness, God called up prophets to both challenge and console.

At times, the prophets described their own call as sudden and dramatic—much like Moses at the burning bush. At other times, the prophets acknowledged that God had been at work from the beginning, slowly shaping them for the task ahead. Jeremiah saw his whole life pointing towards his prophetic vocation. God reminded him: "Before I formed you in the womb I knew you, before you were born I dedicated you, a prophet to the nations I appointed you" (Jer 1:5). The prophetic vocation flows out of the identity of the prophet, the demands of the present, and the love of God who draws these two together.

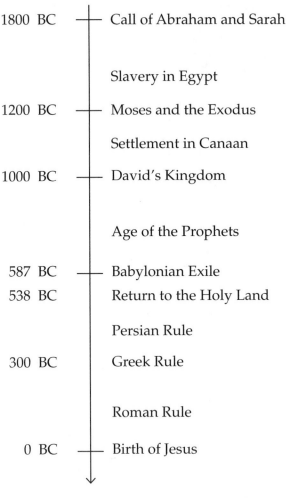

1800 BC	Call of Abraham and Sarah
	Slavery in Egypt
1200 BC	Moses and the Exodus
	Settlement in Canaan
1000 BC	David's Kingdom
	Age of the Prophets
587 BC	Babylonian Exile
538 BC	Return to the Holy Land
	Persian Rule
300 BC	Greek Rule
	Roman Rule
0 BC	Birth of Jesus

Bible Timeline
(approximate dates)

These biblical stories of God's call to individuals are powerful. But they depend on the broader context of God's call to the whole people of Israel. For Israel, God's call is primarily a corporate invitation. It is a communal vocation. God entered into covenant with a people—who became a royal priesthood and a holy nation. "For you are a people holy to the LORD, your God; the LORD, your God, has chosen you from all the peoples on the face of the earth to be a people specially his own" (Deut 7:6). The prophet Isaiah spoke for all of Israel when he said, "Before birth the LORD called me, from my mother's womb he gave me my name" (Isa 49:1). Like Abraham, Moses, and the others, there is nothing Israel did to deserve this special relationship with God. The call came entirely out of God's own love and fidelity. It was pure gift, the grace of being drawn into friendship with God.

While Christians affirm that this gift endures, and that the people of Israel always remain dear to God, Christians also claim in faith that this covenant finds its fulfillment in Jesus Christ. In Christ, God's call to humanity was finally answered in a way that brings salvation to the whole of history and to the entire human family.

The New Testament

At the very beginning of his ministry, Jesus issued a call. Walking by the Sea of Galilee, Jesus saw Simon and Andrew fishing along the shore. He called out to them, "Come after me, and I will make you fishers of men" (Mark 1:17). In the Gospel of Mark, the men responded immediately. They left their nets and followed him. A little later they came across two brothers, James and John, fixing their own fishing nets. Jesus called them. They too dropped everything and followed Jesus.

The Gospel of John, however, suggests a more gradual response to Christ's call. At the very beginning of the gospel, John the Baptist pointed out Jesus to two disciples, "Behold, the Lamb of God." When they approached him, Jesus issued not a command but a question: "What are you looking for?" Here the call of Christ came as an invitation to these two men to reflect on their own experiences and their own deepest desires. They responded only that they wanted to know more, "Rabbi, where are you staying?" Jesus replied, "Come, and you will see" (John 1:38-39). Time with Jesus transformed these men into disciples. They would go out and invite others to come and see.

In these different stories, the same features appear—features we have already seen in the Old Testament stories of call. Discipleship begins not with a choice but with a *call*. This call is a call to *relationship* with Jesus. And this relationship leads to inner *transformation* and outward *mission*.[2]

After Jesus' death, resurrection, and ascension into heaven, the Holy Spirit descended on the apostles. This experience transformed these frightened followers into bold missionaries, who went out to spread the Good News of Christ to the whole world.

One of the most important of these early missionaries was Paul. Paul (or Saul as he was known) was not with the apostles at that first Pentecost. The Acts of the Apostles describes his call coming later, and describes it in dramatic fashion. Saul was literally knocked to the ground as Christ spoke to him from heaven. In a blinding flash, Saul became Paul. In a moment, the enemy became the advocate.

In his own writings, however, Paul described his calling in the language of Isaiah or Jeremiah: "But when [God], who from my mother's womb had set me apart and called me through his grace, was pleased to reveal his Son to me" (Gal 1:15-16). Paul seemed to place his conversion within the longer context of God's plan for his life. Only in hindsight did Paul see what God had always intended for him. Throughout his letters, the notion of call appears again and again. Paul described Jesus as "the one who calls." He referred to Christians as "those who are called." Indeed the New Testament word for "church" is *ekklesia*—which means "the assembly of those who are called." The whole church, and everyone in it, is called to follow Christ.

Variety in Vocation

Everyone has a vocation! After centuries of neglect, Catholics have reclaimed this ancient biblical truth. God calls every single one of us.

Within this inclusive view, we continue to talk about vocation in a variety of ways. Take for example the definition offered by the *United States Catholic Catechism for Adults*:

> Vocation: The term given to the call to each person from God; everyone has been called to holiness and eternal life, especially in Baptism. Each person can also be called more specifically to the priesthood or to religious life, to married life, and to single life, as well as to a particular profession or service.[3]

In this single definition, "vocation" is applied to at least three different levels: the call to holiness and discipleship, the call to a state of life, and the call to serve. These levels are interrelated and often overlap in the life of an individual.

Years ago, two theologians, Marie Theresa Coombs and Francis Kelly Nemeck, OMI, decided that when Catholics talk about vocation they usually use the word in one of these three ways.[4] Vocation can refer to:

1. *Who* God calls me to be,
2. *How* God calls me to live, and
3. *What* God calls me to do.

The first speaks to our *self-identity*, the unique way each of us embodies and lives out the universal call to holiness. The second speaks to our *state of life*, whether that be the ordained, the consecrated, or the lay life. The third speaks to our *ministry*, the particular way each of us is called to serve God and others. All three are important. All three are intertwined. All three come together in the lives of those serving or seeking ways to serve the church as lay ministers.

Who God Calls Me to Be

The Second Vatican Council taught that, prior to any particular vocation, there is a general call to salvation, discipleship, and holiness. Vatican II dedicated an entire chapter of its Dogmatic Constitution on the Church to the "universal call to holiness." There the council proclaimed with confidence: "Therefore, all in the church, whether they belong to the hierarchy or are cared for by it, are called to holiness, according to the apostle's saying: 'For this is the will of God, your sanctification'" (*Lumen Gentium* 39).

For many of us the language of "holiness" can be off-putting. It can evoke images of pious churchgoers or heroic saints. It can seem distant from our ordinary, everyday lives. This is an unfortunate misunderstanding. As Vatican II makes clear, holiness is, at its root, "the perfection of charity" (*Lumen Gentium* 40). The word perfection implies growth. Charity means love. Thus to be holy is *to grow in love*. This is our first and foremost calling. And it extends to all.

But just because the call to holiness is universal does not mean that it is generic. The call extends to all. But it is not the same for everyone.

This point was brought home to me several years ago when I returned to my old high school for my younger sister's graduation.

Before commencement, a baccalaureate mass was held in the white frame church next to the school. All the seniors arrived early wearing their caps and gowns. They processed in at the start of Mass. They filled the pews in front. Several of them served as lectors, gift bearers, and eucharistic ministers.

When it was time for the homily, Fr. Charlie came down from the altar and stood before the seniors. They sat there, proud as peacocks on the day of their graduation, with all of us family and friends beaming behind them.

Father began, "What a beautiful day! What a happy day! There is so much to celebrate and enjoy today."

He continued, "But as your pastor, I feel that it is my responsibility to remind you graduates—on this day—of an important truth."

"Your parents never wanted you."

He said it with a straight face. But we all laughed. And after we quieted down, Fr. Charlie repeated solemnly:

"Your parents never wanted you."

He went on, "Now don't get me wrong, maybe your parents wanted a baby. I am sure they wanted a healthy baby. Maybe they wanted a boy or they wanted a girl."

"But your parents never wanted . . . *you*."

After a pause, he said, "Only *God* wanted . . . *you*."

Father Charlie said it again and again, pointing to each individual graduate in the front row, "Only *God* wanted . . . *you*."

I feel like I have spent almost twenty years now trying to take those words seriously. What does it mean to believe that God wanted . . . *me*? Not me without all my faults and imperfections. Not me without all my insecurities and inner doubts. God wanted *me*. Just as I am.

God's call to me is rooted in God's love for me—a love that is utterly personal. According to our Catholic faith, the billions and billions of human beings spread around the world and scattered across history are not the result of some mass production scheme. We are the astonishing gift of a God who chooses to love again and again and again. Each of us is the result of a unique act of love that has never been seen before and will never be seen again. As the story of Fr Charlie reminds us, God *wants* every single one of us.

Centuries ago, St. Augustine prayed, "By loving me, Lord, you have made me lovable." Discovering *who* God wants me to be begins in a basic act of self-acceptance. God loved me into existence. God not only designed me, God *desired* me. And because of that *I am lovable*.

Too often we imagine God's call as "out there" and apart from us. We treat our vocation as some kind of riddle that we have to decipher or some secret message that we have to decode. Such an approach transforms God's plan into a set of arbitrary instructions—directions for life that are hidden from view.

The twentieth-century spiritual writer Thomas Merton suggested another way. In a brief essay from his collection *Seeds of*

Contemplation, Merton wrote: "For me to be a saint means to be myself." To be holy, Merton argued, is not to imitate someone else's ideal. It is not to look for my vocation "out there." Rather, holiness is the slow unfolding of one's own God-given identity. It is the process of coming to accept the call of God written in my heart before I was born. According to Merton, what separates human beings from the rest of God's creation is that we can *choose* to be what God created us to be. We are free to sin, but sin is simply a turning away from our true self. "Trees and animals have no problem. God makes them what they are without consulting them, and they are perfectly satisfied. With us it is different. God leaves us free to be whatever we like. We can be ourselves or not, as we please."[5]

Discernment, then, is not a spiritual treasure hunt. It is less about looking out and more about listening within. To discover a calling is to hear a certain harmony between *who* I am as a child of God, on the one hand, and *how* I live and *what* I do, on the other. When faith-filled people say that they have discovered their vocation, they are not saying that they found some hidden plan. Rather, they are saying that they have felt a profound resonance between their deepest sense of themselves before God and a particular path forward.

How God Calls Me to Live

Growing up, I often heard the word "vocation." And I always knew what it meant. To "have a vocation" was to be called to be a priest or a nun.

My childhood pastor, Fr. Francis, was always talking about vocations. Every chance he got, he worked it into his homilies. Every visit to our classroom, Father brought it up. Every prayer he led, it seemed, ended with a prayer for vocations.

I later learned that this was unusual. When a new pastor arrived, he did not seem as preoccupied with the subject. Still, Fr. Francis left a lasting impression. On the one hand, his constant preaching about "the vocation crisis" instilled in me a sense that the church needed me—that *God* needed me—and that I had the ability to respond. On the other hand, there seemed to be only one way to respond: become a priest. That was the only vocation that really mattered.

With Vatican II's affirmation of the universal call to holiness, Catholics began to see that there are many ways to respond. There are many vocations that matter. Increasingly, *marriage* was described as a vocation alongside priesthood and religious life—although this often left single people in a kind of no-man's-land. Pope John Paul II offered a more inclusive framework by placing alongside priesthood and religious life the vocation to the *lay life*. His many writings encouraged and affirmed a diversity of callings: married and single, mothers and fathers, young people and old, theologians and political leaders, the sick and those who care for them. But he described three states of life as foundational: "The vocations to the lay life, to the ordained ministry and to the consecrated life can be considered paradigmatic, inasmuch as all particular vocations, considered separately or as a whole, are in one way or another derived from them or lead back to them, in accordance with the richness of God's gift."[6]

In his emphasis on the lay vocation, Pope John Paul II was developing the teaching of the Second Vatican Council. Vatican II stands out from all previous church councils for the attention it gave to the laity. Vatican II affirmed both the essential role of the laity in the life and mission *of the church* and their particular vocation *in the world*. Overcoming centuries of Christian spirituality that had reduced "the world" to a site of sin and temptation, Vatican II saw the world as the positive context that both informs the life of the laity and, in turn, is transformed by their Christian witness.

The laity are *secular*—and that is not a slur. For the secular is understood here not as some godforsaken wasteland separate from the church. Instead, the bishops at Vatican II used the word to talk about ordinary life. In the world of family and friends, work and recreation, politics and culture, God must be present.

[The laity] live in the world, in each and every one of the world's occupations and callings and in the ordinary circumstances

of social and family life which, as it were, form the context of
their existence. There they are called by God to contribute to
the sanctification of the world from within, like leaven, in the
spirit of the Gospel, by fulfilling their own particular duties.
(*Lumen Gentium* 31)

The laity are not left behind as priests and religious go off to
follow their vocations. The laity have their own vocation: to
transform the world in the light of Christ.

This emphasis on the lay vocation in the world should not be
understood in an exclusive sense. And it would be a mistake
to think that Vatican II set up a dichotomy between clergy and
religious "in the church" and laity "in the world." After all, the
council documents describe a number of church ministries for
the laity, just as they admit that priests and nuns sometimes
have secular jobs.

Vatican II's description of the laity in the world has to be read
in the context of its larger teaching that it is *the whole church*, and
not just the laity, that exists "in the world." It is *the whole church*
that has a mission to transform the secular. Vatican II's Pastoral
Constitution on the Church in the Modern World states:

> Thus the church, at once "a visible organization and a spiritual
> community," travels the same journey as all of humanity and
> shares the same earthly lot with the world: it is to be a leaven
> and, as it were, the soul of human society in its renewal by Christ
> and transformation into the family of God. (*Gaudium et Spes* 40)

The whole church is to be leaven in the world. The call of the laity
to transform the secular is thus an intensification of the vocation
of every single member of the Body of Christ.

Some have argued that *lay ministry* should be discouraged
because it is not proper to the lay vocation. Laity belong in the
world, not in the church. Such an argument twists Vatican II's description of the laity into a prohibition that was never intended.
A path more faithful to the council has been suggested by the
U.S. Bishops. Speaking positively of the role of lay ministry in
the church, the bishops wrote:

All of the baptized are called to work toward the transformation of the world. Most do this by working in the secular realm; some do this by working in the Church and focusing on the building of ecclesial communion, which has among its purposes the transformation of the world.[7]

To minister in and on behalf of the church is not to step away from the lay vocation to transform the world. It is simply to serve this mission in a different way.

What God Calls Me to Do

The final question, "*What* does God call me to do?" brings us back to where we began: the call to serve. Here we reflect briefly on what is in fact the concern of the whole book, the vocation to minister as a layperson within and on behalf of the church.

Over a decade ago, a subcommittee of the United States Conference of Catholic Bishops undertook a wide-ranging study of lay ministry. Early on in this process, the bishops arranged a consultation that included several lay ministers who worked on different parish staffs in a variety of ministerial roles. As the conversation unfolded, a few of the lay ministers began to share their experiences of being called to ministry. They spoke of the ways God had worked in their lives, and the ways God was still at work in their lives. They told their vocation stories.

The bishops present were clearly moved by this personal testimony. For some, it was the first time they had heard lay ministers speak about their call to ministry with the same kind of spiritual depth, gratitude, and personal conviction that the bishops were used to hearing from their priests. Afterward, the bishops discussed what they had heard. They asked: Is lay ministry a new vocation in the church? Is it comparable to the call to ordained ministry? Is it more like the consecrated life? How does the call to lay ministry relate to the broader vocation of the laity?

In this exchange, the bishops were being forced to move beyond a notion of vocation as "state of life." They were being stretched by the lived experience of these lay ministers. Lay ministry is not a state of life in the traditional sense. It does not entail the same kind of permanence or totality that has been historically associated with priestly or religious vocations. And yet, these elements are not entirely missing. Many lay ministers *do* make a significant commitment to ministry—some even leave jobs or move in order to take a new ministerial position. Those who minister full-time experience God's call as a life-orienting vocation, one that profoundly impacts their faith, their families, and their future. Those who volunteer or who serve in more occasional or part-time ministries also experience a call. They feel drawn by God to respond to a need or to use a gift. And they describe it in the language of vocation—not a state of life, but a call to serve.

To their credit, the bishops listened. They sought out ways to acknowledge and affirm this new way of talking about vocation. In their initial report, the bishops on the subcommittee wrote:

> Lay ministers speak often and reverently of their call or vocation to ministry, a call that finds its origin in the call of God and its confirmation in the appointment to a specific ministry within the Church. These ministers often experience such a call within, and sometimes transcending, a vocation to married, single, or religious life. . . . We conclude that this call or vocation is worthy of respect and sustained attention.[8]

Such honest reflection offers a glimpse into the way new experiences challenge us as a church, drawing us in new directions. The process is always ongoing.

The end result of the bishops' work was their 2005 document *Co-Workers in the Vineyard of the Lord: A Resource for Guiding the Development of Lay Ecclesial Ministry*. Its particular focus are those lay ministers who have been professionally prepared and who serve in leadership positions, usually on a parish staff, such as directors of religious education, outreach coordinators, pastoral associates, liturgical coordinators, and youth ministers. But the document is sensitive to the variety of different kinds of lay ministries that have taken shape in our time. They affirm these new forms of ministry—claiming that God is at work in calling forth these ministers to serve. The document invites the whole church to continue to work to support and sustain these new vocations to ministry. It calls for greater attention to the formation, authorization, and coordination of lay ministers.

Co-Workers in the Vineyard also reflects on the lay minister's experience of vocation: "The call may come in a dramatic moment. More often, it comes over time, as the person grows— within the community of faith—in love for God and a desire to do his will."[9] Discerning this call, the document continues, is always both a personal and a communal process. Clarity comes through prayer and reflection, as well as through conversations with family, colleagues, and mentors. The document concludes with a call for "a more thorough study of our theology of vocation"—acknowledging that we are still "on the way" toward understanding how God is calling lay ministers to serve the church and the world of today.

Theology for Ministry

Our brief survey of biblical stories suggests four elements of God's call. First, a vocation always arises out of *God's initiative.* It may confront us suddenly or it may grow slowly over time. It may take form in some external need we feel compelled to address, or it may be felt as a deep desire within our hearts. Regardless, no vocation is self-starting. No matter how much it flows through me and is a part of me, my vocation originates beyond me. It is God who calls.

Second, vocation draws us into *relationship* with the triune God. Through Christ and the Spirit, we are drawn into the communion of the Trinity. We accept—in a specific and concrete way—the friendship that God always offers us. We find a particular way to love.

The love that accompanies any genuine vocation leads to personal *transformation* and always extends outward in *mission* toward others—the third and fourth elements of the biblical notion of call. Even the act of accepting oneself as the person God always intended us to be can be a profoundly transformative event. It can realign one's whole life. Even if it doesn't seem to change a thing, it changes everything—deepening a life already well-lived. Usually, interior transformation bursts out into our relationships with other people. God's call moves us to love our neighbor, it sends us forth, it gives us a mission. In his interactions with others, Jesus was always drawing people in and then sending them out. This dynamic continues into the present.

Vocation speaks to various realities—discipleship, state of life, and ministry. The rich way in which these realities come together in the life of an individual points toward an approach to discernment that takes seriously a simple truth: The same God who made us is the same God who saves us. We begin to hear our various callings by reflecting on our true identity, the person God made each of us to be, what Thomas Merton termed the "true self."

Merton knew from his own experience that accepting one's true self can be a difficult journey. He was not naïve about the way in which sin can so easily distort and distract us from our true identity. We so often confuse who God made each of us to be with who *I* want me to be. That is the reality of sin, what Merton called the "false self." In a brief, but beautiful passage, Merton explains that the false self is the attempt to live outside the radius of God's love and will. The great irony, however, is that *nothing* can exist outside the radius of God's love. So the false self is a kind of illusion. It is the attempt to live where there is no life. Sin, then, is self-destruction. It is a denial of who I am.

What the Christian tradition reminds us again and again, however, is that where sin grows, grace overflows (Rom 5:20). And so vocational discernment ultimately comes down to a question: Will I choose to go with the grain of my being or to grate against it? To answer *yes* to God's call is to strike a resounding chord rising out of my deepest and truest self. All authentic and particular vocations flow out of this *yes*.

Coombs and Nemeck suggest that the more we mature, the more the *who*, the *how*, and the *what* of our vocations interconnect.

They compare the three to the interdependence of our lungs, heart, and circulatory system. We may separate one from another for careful examination. But each functions as an essential part of an integrated and complex whole.

Moreover, each of these three dimensions of vocation are themselves multifaceted. My identity (*who* God calls me to be) cannot be summed up in a single, all-encompassing definition. My state of life (*how* God calls me to live) is neither singular nor static. And my ministry (*what* God calls me to do) may not be the same today as it is tomorrow. We grow. The needs of the world and of our church change. Circumstances conspire. And God continues to call.

The chapters that follow are not meant to uncover the "one thing" you were always meant to do. They are not designed to help you discover your once-and-for-all vocation. Rather, these pages hope to draw you into an ongoing process of reflecting on yourself, your life, and your experiences of service in order to appreciate more deeply the God who—through it all—gently calls your name.

For Reflection and Discussion

1. Share your vocation story—the narrative you wrote at the beginning of the chapter. What elements of the biblical pattern of call (divine initiative, personal relationship, inner transformation, and outward mission) are present? What elements are hard to see?

2. Discernment involves listening for harmony between your true self and a particular path forward. Think of a big decision you faced in your life. How did you know what to do? How did you make your decision?

3. What does it mean to be leaven "in the world"? How does your life and ministry serve to transform the world in the light of Christ?

4. How does your state or stage of life influence your ministry? How does your ministry influence the rest of your life?

Recommended Reading

United States Catholic Catechism for Adults (Washington, DC: USCCB Publishing, 2006), chapters 1–4.

Catechism of the Catholic Church, second edition (Vatican City: Libreria Editrice Vaticana, 2000), nn. 26–184.

Hahnenberg, Edward P. *Awakening Vocation: A Theology of Christian Call.* Collegeville, MN: Liturgical Press, 2010.

Pope John Paul II. On the Vocation and the Mission of the Lay Faithful in the Church and in the World (*Christifideles Laici*), http://www.vatican.va/holy_father/john_paul_ii/apost_exhortations/documents/hf_jp-ii_exh_30121988_christifideles-laici_en.html.

Neafsey, John. *A Sacred Voice is Calling: Personal Vocation and Social Conscience.* Maryknoll, NY: Orbis Books, 2006.

Ryan, Robin, ed. *Catholics on Call: Discerning a Life of Service in the Church.* Collegeville, MN: Liturgical Press, 2010.

Second Vatican Council. Dogmatic Constitution on Divine Revelation (*Dei Verbum*), http://www.vatican.va/archive/hist_councils/ii_vatican_council/.

2 By God . . .

It happened in those days that Jesus came from Nazareth of Galilee and was baptized in the Jordan by John. On coming up out of the water he saw the heavens being torn open and the Spirit, like a dove, descending upon him. And a voice came from the heavens, "You are my beloved Son; with you I am well pleased." (Mark 1:9-11)

Jesus felt loved by God—and it launched his ministry.

Surely Jesus knew the Father's love his whole life. When he met John the Baptist at the Jordan River, this love washed over him in a powerful way. As Jesus came up out of the water, he heard his heavenly Father say, "You are precious to me. And I am so proud of you." For the rest of his life, Jesus would share with others the love that he so deeply experienced himself.

"You are my beloved child." God said it to Jesus. God says it to each of us. Every vocation to ministry, every call to serve, begins here.

Starting with Experience

Each of us has our own "Jordan Moment"—that moment that we mark as the beginning of our ministry. It may have been a dramatic decision, a big step in our lives. Or it may have been a gradual process that evolved over time. Either way, there is some story that we can tell about how we got into ministry. It is our vocation story—the way we "heard the call" to serve.

23

In the last chapter, we explored our individual vocation stories. Now we take a moment to back up and think about what led to that call. Long before our "Jordan Moment," each of us came to know God. Each of us came to know God's love.

The church refers to the thirty years between Jesus' birth and his public ministry as the "hidden life" of Christ. It is called "hidden" because we know almost nothing about these years. Most of the time Jesus spent on earth is simply skipped over by the gospel writers. The Gospels of Mark and John begin their stories with John the Baptist. Matthew and Luke share a little about Jesus' birth, but then leap to his adult life. Other than a short story about his trip to the temple at the age of twelve, all we know about this period is that Jesus "advanced [in] wisdom and age and favor before God and man" (Luke 2:52). But it is precisely during these hidden years that Jesus grew to know God's love. What was it like for him?

What was it like for us? We all have our own "hidden life"— that time of childhood, adolescence, and early adulthood when we came to know God and God's love. Usually this love of God is learned through the love of other people. Where have we felt that love in our lives? This may be a difficult—even painful— question to ask. Love often means loss. And joy can easily turn to sorrow. We may have been let down by those who should have loved us from the beginning. We may still be waiting to be accepted and loved as we are. People and events have shaped us from the start. They continue to shape us. How has God worked in our lives?

Pause and reflect on your own experience. How would you describe your own "hidden life"? If it helps, construct a timeline stretching from your birth to today. Chart the highs and the lows, place on it the people who have loved you and the people who have hurt you, and mark both the times when God felt close and the times when God felt far away. Reflect on how God has been at work through it all.

The Experience of God

This chapter introduces the Christian concept of God. And from the start, we have to admit that the topic is overwhelming. How do you talk about the transcendent God? How do you put into words the source of all words? How do you study an infinite reality that escapes and surpasses any finite observation?

While we cannot *examine* God through scientific investigation, our faith claims that we can *experience* God nonetheless. It is this experience that serves as the basis for all theological reflection.

But what is the experience of God like? We saw in the last chapter that divine revelation is not a literal transmission of words, like a phone call or a text message from heaven. Just so, the experience of God is not a physical encounter, as if God steps down through the clouds to greet us. The encounter is deeper, the experience is felt within. It may come through other people or external events, but it touches something inside of us.

One of my favorite assignments is to ask students to write a spiritual autobiography. In a few short pages, I ask them to talk about the most important moments along their faith journey.

I remember one paper in particular. In it, the student described an experience he had during a high school retreat. In the middle of a late-night service that included eucharistic adoration, this young man was overcome with a profound sense of God's forgiveness. This student did not understand where it came from or why. (He wasn't, after all, a bad kid.) He could not give reasons for the experience or defend it academically. He didn't even feel like he could describe it all that well. And yet, he said it was the most real thing he had ever experienced. As he put it, his heart swelled with such joy that he thought his chest would burst. And everything "seemed different" afterwards.

Reflecting on it later, the student said that that moment became a kind of touchstone. It was the most genuine truth he had ever known. It was a "proof" of God's love that he could never prove. He told himself that, should he ever doubt, should he ever get lost or lose sight of what is important in life, he would simply return to that experience and remind himself of what was "most real."

What my student was articulating was a simple, but profound truth: there is more to life than meets the eye. There is "something more" to the world, something that we could never measure or mark out. He was describing an experience more *real* to him than anything science could ever discover.

By no means are such experiences limited to explicitly religious settings. More often than not they burst forth in the midst of our ordinary, day-to-day lives. Psychologists call these "peak experiences," those moments when everything becomes clear, when the whole of life comes together in a unified sense of meaning and purpose. Such peak experiences come as a gift and they spark a sense of gratitude. They are self-validating—that is, the experience justifies itself without any external confirmation or verification. As my student said, it is a proof that you could never prove.

In her novel *Dinner at the Homesick Restaurant*, Anne Tyler describes just such an experience of "something more." The book tells the story of Pearl Tull, who raises three children alone after her husband abandons the family. Toward the end of the story, Pearl, now old and dying, lives with one of her sons, Ezra. Every day Ezra reads to Pearl bits from the diary she kept since childhood. In a scene just before her death, Ezra happens on the following entry and begins to read:

> "*Early this morning,*" he read to his mother, "*I went out behind the house to weed. Was kneeling in the dirt by the stable with my pinafore a mess and the perspiration rolling down my back, wiped my face on my sleeve, reached for the trowel, and all at once thought, Why I believe that at just this moment I am absolutely happy.*"
>
> His mother stopped rocking and grew very still.
>
> "*The Bedloe girl's piano scales were floating out her window,*" he read, "*and a bottle fly was buzzing in the grass, and I saw that I was kneeling on such a beautiful green little planet. I don't care what else might come about, I have had this moment. It belongs to me.*"
>
> That was the end of the entry. He fell silent.
>
> "Thank you, Ezra," his mother said. "There's no need to read any more."[1]

Often such experiences are hard to put into words. They evoke a sense of peace or purpose that defies easy explanation. The theologian Thomas O'Meara shares a story from his own childhood:

> One morning in August, when I was about 13, after I had delivered my 60 or so papers, I was sitting on a hill and noticed the red sun beginning to rise above the steamy woods along the river. I had a feeling I had never experienced before, a feeling that was to return and whose inner conviction had, I thought, a source outside of me. Seeing how good the world and life were, I felt that there was some force moving through that beautiful August morning that wanted to communicate with me. For some reason, that someone did not or could not speak to me in words—but that did not mean it did not exist or was absent. There was something more within the woods, the homes, and the sky—and it was friendly toward me.[2]

The psychiatrist could explain these experiences away in purely scientific terms. They are just the firing of neurons and nerves, the unfolding of complex electrochemical processes within the brain. But the person of faith believes that beyond these processes (and working in some hidden way *through* them) there lies the reality that we call God. For Christians, these human experiences point beyond the physical universe to a transcendent force—a force that is *friendly*. We feel the presence of a *personal God* drawing us into relationship.

As the examples suggest, the experience of God can come through positive moments, such as the silence of prayer, the beauty of nature, or the intimacy of friendship and love. But the experience of God can also come through the negatives of life—tragedy or suffering, helplessness or injustice.

I grew up with a very positive image of God. God was always a loving parent who watched over me and protected me. This idea of God stayed with me into adulthood, laying the foundation for a friendship with God that remains a source of confidence and comfort in my life. However, when my wife and I were first married, we suffered the loss of a miscarriage. And I wondered where God had gone. We were totally devastated.

Where was the God who had always kept us safe? Why would a good friend allow something like this to happen? At the time, it was almost impossible to see God's love in any of it. God just seemed absent.

After a long time, healing came. And, for me, healing came through a slow and growing realization that God *is* a loving parent—a parent who knew exactly what I was going through. One Sunday, looking up at the crucifix in church, it dawned on me: *God knows what it's like to lose a child.* That realization didn't make the pain disappear overnight. But it did help me realize that God had never left. And it led me into a deeper appreciation for God's compassion—a love that shares in our suffering.

The Surprising God of Jesus

According to our Christian faith, the experience of God is an experience of love. In many ways, that is what Jesus spent his whole ministry trying to communicate. His union with the Father gave him an experience of God so profound that no human words could ever fully capture it. Jesus did not set himself the impossible task of trying to explain this love. Instead, he told stories in order to evoke something of its mystery.

Take, for example, the parable of the Prodigal Son (Luke 15:11-32). It is one of Jesus' most famous stories—and one that we almost always mess up. To understand how we so often misunderstand this story, we need look no further than the title of the parable. It's all wrong. The parable is not about the son. It is about the father, and the father's unconditional, overwhelming love.

Remember how the story begins: The younger son went to his father and demanded his share of the father's inheritance. It is important to keep in mind that Jesus' original audience would have been startled—even offended—by such a start. In their world, they knew that it was always the *oldest* son who inherited *all* the family property. For the younger son to expect half would have been ridiculous. He had no right to ask for such a thing. But instead of scolding the son for such a stupid request, the father split up the estate and gave the money to the boy, who went off and wasted all of it.

At this point in the story, the theologian Fr. Michael Himes says, "we know two things: the younger son is thoughtless and self-centered, and the father is a hopelessly irresponsible parent."[3]

It gets worse. After spending all the money, the son decided to go home, where at least he knew he could get a good meal. On his return, the father ran out to embrace him with open arms, showering the younger son with gifts and a great party. Before the boy ever said he was sorry, the father had already welcomed him back. (The text says that the father was moved with love when he saw the son "a long way off"—in other words, *before* they had a chance to speak, *before* the son had a chance to explain himself or offer his apology.) When the older son came in from the field and complained about this unfair treatment, all the father could say was, "We must celebrate and rejoice, because your brother was dead and has come to life again; he was lost and has been found."

We miss the point of the parable when we focus on the son, or pretend the story is about repentance. Here Jesus did not seem particularly interested in the son's repentance. He did not seem particularly interested in the son at all. Jesus was interested in the father. Through the character of the father, Jesus was trying to convey something about God's love for us—total, unconditional, abundant, almost embarrassingly excessive. If "prodigal" means reckless and extravagant, then it is the *father* who is prodigal— prodigal in his love.

It's like Jesus couldn't help himself. He kept searching for the most outrageous way to express how much God loves us. He compared God to a shepherd who abandons ninety-nine sheep to find one stray lamb, or a woman who drops everything to find one lost coin. Such is her joy at finding the coin that she throws a party that almost certainly cost more than the coin she had lost! God makes the sun rise on *everyone*—the evil and the good. God mixes enough dough to feed a village. God scatters

seed all over the place with wasteful abandon—on the road, in
the thorns, over poor soil. God pays the guys who worked just
a couple of hours the same as those who worked all day. All of
these parables that we think are about *us* are really about *God*, a
God whose love spills over like a great flood. In these parables,
you can just imagine Jesus trying to grab us by the shoulders
and shake us awake, desperate to get us up in order to see that
we are drowning in the love of God.

When Jesus met people who were shunned, he touched them
and spent time with them. When he saw people suffering, he
healed them. He taught and lived in ways meant to show people
God's love. Finally, in his death, Jesus told his most important
story about God's love for us: "No one has greater love than this,
to lay down one's life for one's friends" (John 15:13).

God as the Supreme Being

Over fifty years ago the Anglican priest and biblical scholar
J. B. Phillips wrote a short book called *Your God is Too Small*. In
it he argued that the problem with Christianity in our modern
times is not God, but our limited notions about God. According to Phillips, modern Christians had adopted a number of
images that keep God at a distance. Phillips listed a few: God
is the Resident Policeman, a Grand Old Man, or the Managing
Director. God is a great lord or judge, a demanding father-figure,
or a powerful king.

The cumulative effect of these images was to create a huge
chasm between ourselves and God. These images try to make
God sound majestic. But they really make God small, confining
God to our own narrow expectations. They try to limit the radically unlimited God of love that Jesus described in his parables.
If we would only stop trying to put God in a box, Philips argued,
we would open ourselves to the real mystery of the divine.

Phillips was on to something. What he did in his little book
was to put into simple language a complex theological shift that
goes back almost three hundred years.

During the 17th and 18th centuries, European thinkers began to argue that science and human reason were the most reliable way of discovering truth about the world. Believing that they had thrown off the dark superstitions of the past, these intellectuals christened this new era the Age of Enlightenment. The Enlightenment created a crisis for the church and ultimately changed the way Christians thought about God.

The story goes like this: key to the new scientific method of the Enlightenment was the assumption that every observable *effect* had to have an observable *cause*. The whole universe, the scientists concluded, was a closed system of cause and effect. Everything that happens within this system can be explained by exploring its causes—explanations that are best derived through scientific observation and experimentation.

God, however, cannot be observed or measured by the tools of science. God does not fit within the closed system that makes up the universe. Therefore, Enlightenment thinkers concluded, God must be *outside* the system. God must stand apart from the world looking in.

Thus we get the famous metaphor of God as the divine watchmaker. Since God has to be totally separate from the closed universe of cause and effect, at most God is the one who creates the world, winds it up, and then lets it run. This view is known as *Deism*, the idea that God creates the world, but then abandons it to itself. From Deism, it is a short walk to *materialism*, the view that the material world is all that exists. Why do you need a God when the universe seems to get along pretty well on its own?

You can imagine the crisis this caused within the church. And unfortunately the theologians who struggled to respond did not help. In fact, they made a series of fatal mistakes in their effort to defend the faith. To begin with, in mounting their defense, theologians actually adopted many of the same assumptions of their scientifically-minded critics. God was one more thing that could be investigated; faith was one more set of facts that could be proved. The effect was to reduce God to one more "being" alongside other beings. God, they believed, was the "Supreme Being."

In the end, the theologians promoted a view of God that was not all that different from their Deist opponents. Both groups imaged God as separate from and external to the world. The only difference was that the Deists believed that the Supreme Being acted just once in creating the world, while the theologians argued that the Supreme Being continued to act in the world after creation.

But here is the problem. To call God a "Supreme Being" actually belittles God, because it presumes there is a group of things or a class (namely, "all beings") to which God belongs. Even if God is the biggest and best member of that class, God still belongs to a class. God is a part of something *that is bigger than God*. And that is precisely what Christianity rejects. If God is really God, then God cannot be a member of any class.

When I try to draw the model of God as a Supreme Being on the chalkboard, it looks something like the image below.

The trouble with this picture is the chalkboard. By drawing God *on* the chalkboard, I have placed God *in* a frame of reference larger than God. The model puts God (the *supreme* being) in a

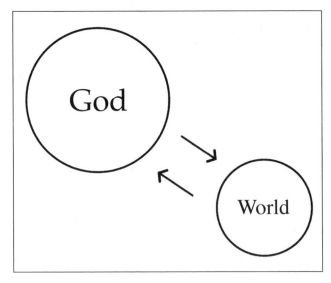

God as the Supreme Being

category (the category of "beings") that transcends God. But nothing transcends God. God can't be *in* a framework—God *is* the framework. Another model is needed.

God as the Dynamism of Love

The model of God as the Supreme Being is a far cry from the understanding of God found in the Bible and maintained by Christians for over a thousand years. For the people of the Bible, God was radically *above* the world, but constantly at work *within* it. Creator and creation were *distinct*, but never *separate*.

In order to appreciate the biblical view of God, we have to keep in mind that, for these ancient believers, the relationship between heaven and earth was much more fluid. They did not share the modern view of the universe as a closed system of cause and effect. They did not see a stark separation between the natural and the supernatural. The boundaries between the two were porous.

My favorite example of this fluidity is the Hebrew word *ru'ah*. *Ru'ah* means "spirit." It also means "breath." It also means "wind." We tend to think of *spirit* as very different from *breath* or *wind*. That is because we have learned to treat the world as a closed system of physical cause and effect. Breath and wind are within the system. Spirit is outside of it. But for the ancient mind, these were of a piece. *Ru'ah* referred to any unseen force that moves and gives life. Thus the spirit of a person and the breath of a person were not so separate. The spiritual and the material were intertwined. God, the awesome power that transcended all earthly powers, was constantly at work in the world.

But didn't this confuse the Creator with creation? Didn't this mix up God and people? No, because what the biblical authors intuitively understood—and what medieval theologians rigorously argued—was that God and the world operate on two radically different planes. They are not two different members of the same class. They are not even two different classes! Rather the world is a class, and God is the infinite context within which all classes are brought into being and sustained in existence.

Here we are moving into deep theological waters. But think in terms of a very simple analogy. When I go to the grocery store, I find a variety of apples for sale. Usually the different varieties are separated on the stand by some kind of plastic or cardboard divider. The divider keeps the Macintosh apart from the Galas, and the Galas apart from the Granny Smiths.

I think we often fall into the trap of imagining God along the model of the apple stand. God is "the Big Apple," separated from all of us little apples by some kind of cosmic divider. That is exactly what the modern idea of God as a "Supreme Being" does. It presents God as an apple that is so much bigger and better *than us*, but still, in the end, an apple *like us*. It fails to capture how radically God transcends the world.

If we are looking for a true analogy, it cannot be one that compares us to little apples and God to a big apple (or even a big orange, or a big melon). A better analogy is this: If we are like apples, then God is like the grocery store . . . or the orchard . . . or the whole process of life and growth that makes every kind of fruit possible.

Thus we might replace our chalkboard sketch of God as the Supreme Being with the following image:

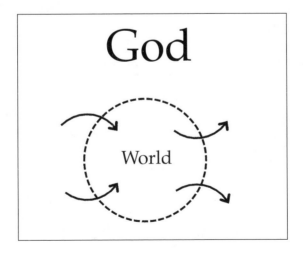

God as the Dynamism of Love

In this diagram, God is not on the chalkboard. God *is* the chalk-board—a chalkboard that stretches out infinitely in every direc-tion. The world falls within the infinite context that is God. By "the world," we mean the realm of creation—everything that the tools of science can examine and explore. It is the entirety of human history, of civilizations come and gone, of the millions of years of life developing on this planet and the millions of years yet to come. It is the whole universe with its billions of galaxies, and trillions of stars, all racing outward at dazzling speed. All of it is encompassed by the Creator. All of it falls within God's loving embrace.

Here we start to brush up against the mystery of God. All that we will ever discover in this universe is but a tiny island in the midst of the infinite ocean that is God. But the analogy lags. For we are not cut off from the sea by the shoreline, keeping the tide at bay. Rather, God's presence encircles us, rains down on us, springs up from below to water the land. God's presence sustains us in being. It is the life-giving water that permeates every living thing. We may exist. But God is the source of our existence. And so God is present to every atom and molecule of the universe—not only having brought it into being, but at every moment sustaining it in existence. In a marvelous paradox, it is the radical *distinction* between Creator and creation that allows for such radical *intimacy* between God and us.

Rediscovering this ancient truth has allowed a number of contemporary theologians to escape the dead end of imaging God as the Supreme Being, and to turn instead to another model, which I call God as the Dynamism of Love. I believe the image of love is not only more faithful to Jesus' own surprising vision of God, but it also recaptures some of the wisdom that has long been a part of the Catholic theological tradition.

Centuries before the Enlightenment, Christian theologians recognized the problems we have been discussing. For example, the great medieval theologian St. Thomas Aquinas saw that it was foolish to think of God on the model of a Supreme Being. To make this point, Aquinas refused to call God *ens*, the Latin word for "a being." Instead he described God with the word *esse*, which is the infinitive form of the verb "to be." God is not "a being." God is simply "to be"—the very power of being—the one who brings everything else into being and sustains it in existence.[4]

Interestingly, in choosing the word *esse* over *ens*, Aquinas was in effect saying: It is better to think of God as a verb than as a noun. God is action, movement, a force moving through the world. Here is another reason to speak of God as the Dynamism of Love, because *love* is a verb. Love is an action and a way of relating. The First Letter of John proclaims: "God is love" (1 John 4:8, 16). John does not call God a *lover*. That would be a noun. Instead, John uses a verb—*God is love*.

The Trinity: God is Love

All that has been said so far in this chapter has been said by way of introducing one of the most central of all Christian beliefs: the doctrine of the Trinity.

The Trinity remains one of the most difficult beliefs of Christianity. It is also one of the most important. At the very beginning of our Christian lives, we were baptized, "In the name of the Father, and of the Son, and of the Holy Spirit." Every time we begin prayer, we make the sign of the cross and say, "In the name of the Father, and of the Son, and of the Holy Spirit." At Mass each Sunday, we profess a Creed composed of three paragraphs, one for each person of the Trinity: "I believe in one God, the Father almighty, maker of heaven and earth. . . . I believe in one Lord Jesus Christ. . . . I believe in the Holy Spirit. . . ." It is not an exaggeration to say that the doctrine of the Trinity is not one belief among many. It is the very structure or framework for *all* our beliefs.

That is why it is sad that so many of us don't really understand the doctrine of the Trinity. In fact, we don't even *expect* to understand it. It is, after all, a mystery!

However, as a number of theologians have recently begun to point out, the doctrine of the Trinity is not a mystery. *God* is the mystery. The doctrine of the Trinity is simply the church's limited way of trying to express this mystery.

The *United States Catholic Catechism for Adults* explains that when we use the word *mystery* for God, we don't mean it in the sense of a detective story or a scientific puzzle. The mystery of God is not something that we figure out through investigation or "solve." God is a mystery that deepens the closer we get to it. It is not like a puzzle, but more like love. The more we grow in love, the more we are amazed and humbled by it, the more we realize that we cannot totally capture it in words. It remains a mystery no matter how deeply we know it.

Over the centuries Christians have searched for analogies to describe the mystery of God as three divine persons in one divine nature. Legend has it that St. Patrick used a shamrock to spread the faith: three leaves in one leaf. Saint Augustine famously compared the Trinity to the human mind, composed of three aspects: memory, intellect, and will. A student once said in class, "This isn't so tough. I just think of my dad. He's one person who is a son *and* a brother *and* a father."

In trying to understand the Trinity, it may be helpful to begin with how we got the doctrine in the first place. It all goes back to Jesus. Those who knew Jesus were deeply touched by him. They had such a powerful experience of God's love in Jesus that they dedicated their lives to him. They spread his message. And the church was born.

But there is more. Those first followers of Jesus did not only experience God's love through Jesus. They experienced God in him. And they felt that presence even after he was gone.

Naturally, it took some time to figure out how to put all of this into words. Jesus never used the word "Trinity." He prayed *to* the Father, but he also said that "The Father and I are one." The first disciples were all Jewish, and their experience of Jesus could easily have led them to deny the monotheism of their faith. But they insisted that God remains one. At the same time, they knew, Jesus was not just a man. Gradually, the church developed a coherent and intellectually sophisticated way of affirming the full divinity of Father, Son, and Spirit—without leading to a belief in three Gods. It is a definition that we repeat every Sunday when we proclaim the Creed.

According to the *United States Catholic Catechism for Adults*, the doctrine of the Trinity can be summarized in three claims. First, the Trinity is one. What the Creed says of the Son is true of the Spirit as well: they are "consubstantial" with the Father. They are of the same substance, of the same essence, "one in being." This clear affirmation of absolute monotheism—one God—is basic to the doctrine. Second, the divine persons are distinct from one another. And, third, the divine persons are in relation to one another. Together, what points two and three affirm is that the persons of the Trinity are distinct precisely in the way that they relate to each other: "The Father cannot be the Father without the Son, nor can the Son be the Son without the Father. The Holy Spirit is related to the Father and the Son who both send him forth."[5]

Obviously, none of this works if we use the word "person" in reference to the divine persons in the same way we use it when we talk about human persons. To do so would be to fall into a belief in three Gods. The ancient Creeds use the word "person" in an entirely different way. And here lies the simple key that makes the doctrine of the Trinity work: the word "person" refers not to an individual, but to a *relationship*.

The doctrine of the Trinity is not the absurdity of an impossible math problem. It is not saying that there are three things in one thing. Rather, it is saying that there are three relations that constitute the one God. Thomas Aquinas captures this truth with typical brevity when he defines the divine persons as "subsistent relations."[6] The divine persons are simply a "relating." God is more like a verb than a noun.

God is love. Books about the Trinity have poured out over the centuries. The best of them affirm this basic insight. If the doctrine emerged out of the effort to describe the disciples' experience of God in Jesus, then the doctrine cannot be understood apart from God's decision to become human. What the Doctrine of the Trinity tells us is that God chooses to enter into relationship with us. God is interested in us. God wants to be our friend.

God wants to enter into loving communion with every single one of us and with all of creation.

This act of loving us reveals the very nature of God. God not only enters into relationship, *God is relationship*. The doctrine of the Trinity makes clear that God is not a solitary ego, nor a club of three. God is the dynamic *communion*—the *love*—among Father, Son, and Spirit. Or, as the *Catechism of the Catholic Church* puts it so beautifully: "God's very being is love. By sending his only Son and the Spirit of Love in the fullness of time, God has revealed his innermost secret (cf. 1 Cor 2:7-16; Eph 3:9-12): God himself is an eternal exchange of love, Father, Son, and Holy Spirit, and he has destined us to share in that exchange" (CCC 221).[7] God is a fundamentally relational reality, a loving communion that spills over, reaching out and drawing us into the divine life.

The great African American theologian Howard Thurman observed that you cannot argue your way into this idea. You cannot deduce it or figure it out on your own. It comes as a gift: "This is the great disclosure: that there is at the heart of life a Heart."[8]

We can only begin to imagine the implications of this trinitarian understanding of God. If God is fundamentally relational—a dynamism of loving communion—and if we, as human beings, are created "in the image and likeness of God," then we too must be fundamentally relational beings. What a contrast to our individualistic society! We are made not to be alone, but to be in communion with God and with others. This insight ought to touch every aspect of our lives. It will have significant implications for how we understand our call to ministry.

New Images of God

We have been describing God as a verb, a presence, or an infinite ocean engulfing our lives. Do these new images replace the images of God we learned growing up? Not at all. But we are invited to complement these older images with new ones.

Our early images of God can be a source of deep consolation. They can also be negative and damaging to our relationship with God. If God is the infinite Dynamism of Love, we always have to keep asking: How *loving* is my image of God? We will also have to recognize that no one image can ever fully grasp the mystery of God. We *need* multiple metaphors, because each image points to some aspect of the mystery.

There is a story about a famous feminist theologian who invited a group of colleagues over for dinner with her family. As was their custom, she asked her youngest daughter to say grace. The girl, rather shy among all the strange adults, sheepishly asked her mom, "Do I say the old prayer or the new prayer?"

The theologian replied to her daughter, "It's okay. You can say the old one."

So the girl folded her hands, closed her eyes, and recited, "God is great. God is good. And we thank *her* for this food."

The surprised guests later teased their host: If that was the *old* prayer, they wanted to hear the *new* one!

The idea of God as a Dynamism of Love frees us for *new* ways of relating to God. In recent years, feminist theologians have helped all of us see the many possibilities for thinking and speaking about God that emerge from the lived experience of women. Working within the church and in faithfulness to the tradition, these theologians have pointed out that the image of God as a patriarchal male—the white-haired old man who rules over creation—is not the only way to picture God. They have shown how Jesus himself spoke of God in decidedly nonpatriarchal ways. God is not a domineering disciplinarian who imposes his will on weak children. Rather, God is a concerned parent, a humble servant. Even when Jesus addressed God as Father, he did so with surprising intimacy, calling God *Abba*, or "Daddy." In his parables, Jesus imagined God as a mother hen gathering all her chicks under her wings. He spoke of God as a baker woman kneading the dough, as a housekeeper searching for her lost coin. Centuries of exclusive focus on male images of God have blinded us to the diversity of ways Jesus himself tried to convey the love of God.

Above I used the image of a circle on a chalkboard or an island in the sea to try to convey how the world comes to be within the mystery of God. But isn't a much more appropriate metaphor that of a pregnant mother? When we imagine God creating the world, we tend to think of a craftsman or a potter, fashioning something apart from himself. But to imagine God's creating as a pregnancy invites us toward a much more intimate understanding. Just as a woman's body makes way, opening up space for the new life growing within, so God opens up space for something new. God pulls back and allows something other than God to be. This "something"—all of creation—is its own being, having its own identity and life. But it could not exist were it not sustained in being within the womb of God. As St. Paul preached so long ago, it is in God that we "live and move and have our being" (Acts 17:28).

"God is our father; even more God is our mother." These are not the words of some famous feminist theologian, but of Pope John Paul I, who spoke them near the end of his very brief reign, over thirty years ago. The Pope evoked the tender love of a mother caring for her sick child. He used it to speak of a world sick with war: "If children are ill, they have additional claim to be loved by their mother. And we too, if by chance we are sick with badness and are on the wrong track, have yet another claim to be loved by the Lord."[9] His remark offered an expansive and inclusive way of talking about God—not new to the tradition—which finds an echo in the *Catechism of the Catholic Church*: "God's parental tenderness can also be expressed by the image of motherhood (cf. Isa 66:13; Ps 131:2), which emphasizes God's immanence, the intimacy between Creator and creature" (CCC 239). Since our limited human words can never fully capture the infinite mystery of God, we are always searching for ways to express the incredible scope and profound depth of God's love for us.

Theology for Ministry

The pages above draw on church teaching and recent theological reflection to describe the triune God as a Dynamism of

Love. The God of Christianity is not some Supreme Being detached and disinterested in the world—a God who is, as James Joyce imagined him, removed and paring his fingernails. No, the love that is God permeates the whole world, reaches into every corner of our lives, and sustains us in our very existence. This power of love spreads across all of human history and touches every human heart. As St. Augustine put it so long ago, "God is closer to me than I am to myself."

What implications does this understanding of God have for our ministry? The theologian Richard Gaillardetz offers two insights.

First, in reflecting on the limited notion of God as a Supreme Being, Gaillardetz points out a potential pastoral problem. If we see God as an individual being alongside other individual beings (even if God is the most *supreme* being), then we might easily fall into a kind of competition between God and everything else in life. My attention will be divided. And the spiritual life will become an endless tug-of-war between the things that demand my attention during the day—commuting to work, buying groceries, playing with my children, talking to my spouse—and my religious duties to God.[10] This view leads us to imagine relating to God *alongside* our daily activities, but not *in and through* our daily activities.

Imagining God as the Dynamism of Love helps us to remember that God permeates our lives. There is no aspect of our day-to-day activity that is untouched by the care and concern of God. There can be no competition between my love for my spouse and my love for God. There can be no competition between my response to my children and my response to God. As we saw in the first chapter, Vatican II's affirmation of the "secular character" of the laity was not meant to put down the laity. It was meant to lift up the secular. It was meant to affirm the call to holiness that comes *in and through* the lay person's life in the world. A spirituality for the lay minister cannot separate out home life from church service, but rather seeks out a new kind of synthesis. Activity within both the church and the world offers the opportunity for spiritual growth. Prayer does not sit alongside the rest of our lives—a welcome respite or an occasional injection of God into the day. Prayer is an opportunity to pause so that we can become more fully aware of the God who is always already present.

Gaillardetz's second insight takes this spirituality of the lay minister and turns it toward the work of ministry. In a creative way, he calls the minister a *mystagogue*.[11] Those who are familiar with the Rite of Christian Initiation of Adults recognize the term "mystagogy" as referring to that period following the Easter Vigil when the newly baptized are drawn even further into the mystery of the faith. Other members of the community help these new Christians to understand and appreciate more fully their new baptismal identity. In the early church, mystagogy was a time of post-baptismal catechesis, an opportunity to unpack the "mysteries" (the rituals) that had been celebrated. The idea was that you could not really understand something until you had experienced it yourself. Even then, you needed help to reflect on what had happened in order to see how God was at work.

By calling the minister a mystagogue, Gaillardetz is suggesting that the minister's role today is to help people "unpack" their experience in order to see how God is at work. One of the perpetual mistakes ministers make is to assume that we bring God to people. Would be that we were so quick! If God is the Dynamism of Love that permeates the whole world, then we do not *bring* God to people. God beats us there! God is already at work in the lives of those among whom we minister. Our ministry serves to remind people of this incredible mystery.

For Reflection and Discussion

1. Share the timeline of your "hidden life." What patterns stand out? How has your relationship with God changed over the years?

2. Have you ever had a "peak experience," a moment of peace and clarity when the whole of life seemed to make sense? What was it like? How did it affect your life?

3. How was the doctrine of the Trinity explained to you growing up? How was it similar and how was it different from the explanation here? If you had to give a short introductory presentation on the Trinity to a group of high school students, what would you say?
4. Do you think it is appropriate to use female images and metaphors for God? Is it appropriate in personal prayer? In public liturgies? Why or why not?

Recommended Reading

United States Catholic Catechism for Adults (Washington, DC: USCCB Publishing, 2006), chapters 5–6.

Catechism of the Catholic Church, second edition (Vatican City: Libreria Editrice Vaticana, 2000), nn. 185–324.

Downey, Michael. *Altogether Gift: A Trinitarian Spirituality*. Maryknoll, NY: Orbis Books, 2000.

Gaillardetz, Richard R. *A Vision of Pastoral Ministry*. Liguori, MO: Liguori, 2002.

Himes, Michael J. *Doing the Truth in Love: Conversations about God, Relationships and Service*. Mahwah, NJ: Paulist Press, 1995.

Johnson, Elizabeth A. *She Who Is: The Mystery of God in Feminist Theological Discourse*. New York: Crossroad, 1992, 2002.

3 Through Christ . . .

He came to Nazareth, where he had grown up, and went according to his custom into the synagogue on the sabbath day. He stood up to read and was handed a scroll of the prophet Isaiah. He unrolled the scroll and found the passage where it was written:

> "The Spirit of the Lord is upon me,
>   because he has anointed me
>   to bring glad tidings to the poor.
> He has sent me to proclaim liberty to captives
>   and recovery of sight to the blind,
>   to let the oppressed go free,
> and to proclaim a year acceptable to the Lord."

Rolling up the scroll, he handed it back to the attendant and sat down, and the eyes of all in the synagogue looked intently at him. He said to them, "Today this scripture passage is fulfilled in your hearing." (Luke 4:16-21)

In his very first sermon, Jesus summed up his entire mission and ministry. Everything his life would be about was foreshadowed in this remarkable passage. Good news for the poor! Sight for the blind! Freedom for the oppressed! All of this, Jesus proclaimed, begins today.

We learn a lot about Jesus in this opening scene from Luke's gospel. First, we discover a man deeply rooted in his own Jewish tradition. He attended synagogue on the Sabbath and was

45

familiar with the sacred scriptures of his faith. He recalled the promises of God from of old. Second, Jesus understood his message as a message of hope directed to those who need it most—those who suffer, those in poverty, those ground down by life, those with the most reason to despair. And finally, Jesus saw all of this fulfilled in his own person. He was the one to bring freedom and new life.

Jesus' first sermon opened out into many more. He went on to preach and to teach. He gathered disciples. He healed the sick, welcomed sinners, and challenged the unjust.

He also met resistance. We see it already in this scene. After reading from the scroll of Isaiah, Jesus sat down. With all eyes on him, he boldly proclaimed, "Today this scripture is fulfilled." The people began to doubt. They asked, "How can this be? We've know him since he was a kid. What good is he? What proof can he show us?" When Jesus challenged their narrow vision, the crowd was filled with fury. They drove him out of town and tried to hurl him off a cliff. Jesus' good news was not accepted by all. His life of ministry led to his death on the cross. This too is part of his story.

Starting with Experience

Who hasn't heard of Jesus? Even in our increasingly secular society, it is rare to come across someone who doesn't know *something* about Jesus. Indeed, Jesus is one of the most famous people ever to have lived. His story has circled the globe, making its way into remote lands and diverse civilizations. It has penetrated almost every aspect of western culture, from our art and architecture to our politics and pastimes. Today we encounter the story of Jesus not just in church, but in popular movies, bestselling books, and a seemingly infinite number of websites, blogs, and online groups run by believers and non-believers alike. It is safe to say that many, many people know about Jesus.

But how many people *know* Jesus? The biblical scholar Donald Senior makes an important distinction. *To know about* someone is to be in possession of certain facts about the person. It is to have certain information. What is her name? Where is she from? What does she do? In contrast, *to know* someone is to be drawn into the mystery of the person. It is to be drawn into a relationship, a relationship of friendship and trust.[1]

Pause and reflect on your own experience. How do you know Jesus? How do you relate to him? If it helps, begin by reflecting on your mental picture of the man. What does he look like? How does he act? What are three or four adjectives you would use to describe him? Where did these ideas or images come from? You might collect different pictures that have made an impression on you over the years—famous paintings or simple statues, scenes from the gospels or from movies you have seen. Search online. Reflect on why you find these particular images meaningful and how they reflect your relationship with Jesus.

Learning about Jesus

The point of our Christian faith is that we come to *know* Jesus more and more intimately. The goal is to deepen a relationship. One way to do this is to come to know more *about* Jesus. Like getting to know a good friend, we want to learn more about Jesus' background, his family and his friends, his likes and his dislikes, his deepest desires and his biggest dreams.

The area of theology that strives to *know about* Jesus is called Christology (which means "the study of Jesus Christ"). This chapter offers an introduction to Christology, and like every area of theology Christology ultimately goes back to an experience. In this case, it is the experience of those first disciples who knew the man Jesus of Nazareth. It was his life that inspired their lives. It was his ministry that motivated their own.

For some strange reason, as Christian history unfolded, theologians paid less and less attention to the actual life of Jesus.

They grew preoccupied with abstract questions about how God became human or how Jesus' death on the cross saves us from sin. This preoccupation shaped the Creeds professed on Sunday, the lessons taught in schools, and the prayers said at home.

Take for example the Nicene Creed, a confession of faith that goes back to the fourth century and one that we recite every Sunday at Mass. Pay attention next time and you will notice something curious. In the second paragraph—the paragraph dedicated to our belief in Jesus—the Creed jumps straight from Jesus' birth to Jesus' death. So quick you might miss it, the Creed skips over the thirty years Jesus spent walking the earth! It says nothing about his teaching, his miracles, or his public ministry.

There are good historical reasons why the Creed reads the way it does, reasons we cannot go into here. However, this lack of interest in Jesus' life filtered all the way down to how the faith was taught to children. In the famous *Baltimore Catechism*, which was widely used in the United States up until the 1960s, almost no attention is given to the life of Jesus. Of its 421 questions and answers, only two treat Jesus' earthly ministry. The question, "On what day was Christ born?" is followed just four questions later with "On what day did Christ die?"

Another example is the rosary. This traditional Catholic devotion was arranged according to three sets of "mysteries"—the "Joyful Mysteries" connected to Jesus' birth, the "Sorrowful Mysteries" of his death, and the "Glorious Mysteries" surrounding his resurrection. Again, the Catholic tendency to skip over Jesus' earthly ministry can be seen in the fact that the last Joyful Mystery, the finding of the twelve-year-old Jesus in the Temple, is followed immediately by the first Sorrowful Mystery, the agony in the garden of Gethsemane.

Happily, in our own time, the church has reclaimed the importance of Jesus' life and ministry. The *Catechism of the Catholic Church*, issued in 1992, acknowledges that the Creed speaks only of incarnation and redemption, but argues that these realities do not exhaust the life of Jesus. It goes on to flesh out the mysteries of Jesus' time growing up, his baptism and temptation in the desert, his preaching and his miracles, his transfiguration and his journey to Jerusalem (CCC 512–570). Late in his pontificate, Pope John Paul II, whose devotion to Mary was deep, actually updated the rosary. He added a fourth set of mysteries, the "Luminous Mysteries," precisely to draw attention to the public ministry of Jesus. The rosary now includes meditations on Jesus' baptism, his miracle at Cana, his preaching of the kingdom of God, his transfiguration, and the Last Supper.

This recovery of the life and ministry of Jesus was the fruit of the church's rediscovery of the Bible. Over the past fifty years, Catholics have turned to the gospels with new interest and energy. And in doing so, we have learned so much more about Jesus than ever before.

Turning to the Gospels

The Second Vatican Council's Dogmatic Constitution on Divine Revelation (*Dei Verbum*) calls the four gospels the very heart of the Bible. They are our principle source for learning about the life and teaching of Jesus.

While Vatican II affirmed that the gospels tell us the truth about Jesus, it also acknowledged that the gospels cannot be read as the simple and straightforward accounts of eyewitnesses. And so as we turn to the gospels in order to know more about Jesus, we have to be sensitive to the complex way in which these texts came to be written.

At the time of Vatican II, the Pontifical Biblical Commission (the experts who advise the pope on biblical matters) produced an important document titled "The Historical Truth of the Gospels." Its basic conclusions were incorporated into the final version of *Dei Verbum* and later repeated by the *Catechism of the Catholic Church* (CCC 126). In these documents, the church makes an important point: the gospels evolved. They developed through a process that can be described in three stages: (1) the life of Jesus, (2) oral tradition, and (3) the actual writing of the gospels.

The first stage was the lifetime of Jesus. In naming this stage, the church affirms that the gospels are rooted in history. They are not myths or pure fabrications. They can be traced back to the historical figure Jesus of Nazareth, who lived in the land of Palestine in the first third of the first century. At the same time, the church recognizes that the gospels were not written during this stage. The apostles did not follow Jesus around with note-pads, jotting down everything he said and did.

In fact, before anything was written down the stories of Jesus were passed on by word of mouth. This was the second stage, the period of oral tradition. During this stage, several things happened. First, some of what Jesus said or did was simply forgotten. It is sad, but true. We will never know everything about Jesus that his first disciples knew. Second, those stories that were saved were all, in some way, changed. As stories were told over and over again they were simplified and streamlined, reduced to the bare bones, with details kept to a minimum. Fi-nally, the stories that were saved and simplified gradually be-came detached from one another. They became free-floating and relatively self-contained little narratives. The different stories about Jesus were remembered, but their precise order was not.

The third stage represents the actual composition of the gos-pels. At this stage—which probably began about forty years after Jesus' death—four different authors, living in different places, and writing for different communities, gathered together these disconnected stories. Each author wove them into his own story about the life of Jesus, giving us the Gospels of Matthew, Mark, Luke, and John.

In constructing their gospels, each of the sacred authors had to choose how to arrange the pieces he had inherited and what he would emphasize. These choices were guided by his own inspired vision, but also by the context and needs of the specific community for whom he was writing. My image for this whole process is that of a mosaic. A mosaic is a work of art constructed out of thousands of tiny colored stones. If we imagine stage one of this process of gospel composition as a beautiful multicol-ored statue of Jesus, then stage two represents the shattering of this statue into many small pieces. Each piece represent an individual story about Jesus—a miraculous healing, a short parable, an exchange with a disciple or a Pharisee. As these pieces were passed on from Christian to Christian, the rough edges were smoothed out. The stories became stylized and simplified. In stage three, the four gospel authors collected these stones. Each author glued them together into his own beautiful mosaic of Jesus. Each is unique, and none could ever compare to the original statue. But still, in their colors and textures, in their common patterns and tones, we catch a glimpse of the original, and are led into its beauty.

The image of the mosaic allows us to distinguish between the overall picture each gospel author is trying to present and the individual pieces that serve as the building blocks. Biblical scholars study both. In doing so, they learn both about the historical figure Jesus of Nazareth and about the developing faith of the early church. Our interest for the moment are the pieces, which point

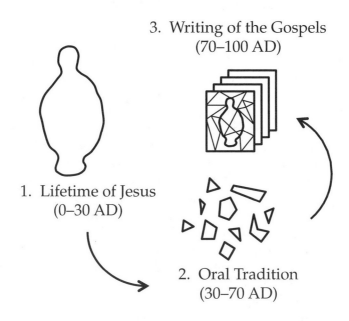

3. Writing of the Gospels
(70–100 AD)

1. Lifetime of Jesus
(0–30 AD)

2. Oral Tradition
(30–70 AD)

Stages in the Composition of the Gospels

us toward the historical Jesus. In tracing these pieces back through the three stages, scholars are able to say quite a lot about the ministry of Jesus of Nazareth—a ministry so important for our own.

What Jesus Said

We begin with Jesus' ministry of preaching and teaching. Scholars are in almost unanimous agreement that the central theme of Jesus' preaching was *the kingdom of God*. The idea of the kingdom of God was not original to Jesus. It had deep roots in the religious history of Israel.

From the promise that Abraham would be the father of a great nation, to the escape from slavery in Egypt, to the establishment of the monarchy under King David—running throughout the Old Testament is a story of hope. God will protect Israel, vanquish her enemies, and establish peace and prosperity among all her people.

All of this seemed within grasp at the time of King David. But the glories of his kingdom were short-lived, and eventually the Israelites met defeat, becoming the subjects of one foreign power after another. In the context of destruction and despair, the prophets kept alive the image of the kingdom of God in order to profess their unshaking faith that, one day, God would come to rule over all the earth. Then, all would be made well.

When Jesus preached the coming of the kingdom of God he was tapping into a rich tradition. But what did Jesus himself mean by the kingdom, or reign, of God? Two extremes are sometimes suggested. A few modern critics have argued that Jesus preached a *this-worldly* kingdom. Jesus called for a political revolution to overthrow the Romans and reestablish the monarchy begun by King David. In this effort he failed miserably and was executed for treason against the state. Others argue the opposite extreme: Jesus spoke only of an *other-worldly* kingdom. The kingdom of God, according to this view, was heaven—a place of peace and happiness in the next life.

Neither of these views fully captures what Jesus' preaching was all about. In his proclaiming, "The kingdom of God is at hand. Repent, and believe in the gospel" (Mark 1:15), Jesus seemed to suggest that the kingdom involved both this-worldly and other-worldly dimensions. Neither purely political nor totally spiritualized, the reign of God evoked the hope of ancient Israel for a time in which God's blessings abound. According to Jesus, the kingdom had arrived, and was yet to come. It is of this world *and* of the next. Above all, the kingdom marks *God's special presence in the world*—a presence and a power that takes everything wrong and makes it right.

Jesus did not lecture about the kingdom of God. Instead, he told stories. And he gave strange examples. The reign of God is like a mustard seed that grows into a great weed (Matt 13:31-32). It is like yeast that taints everything (Matt 13:33). It is like the invitation to a great party that people foolishly refuse (Matt 22:1-14). In these parables Jesus was trying to shock his listeners into recognizing the surprising way in which God is present among us—always demanding a response.

In Jesus' preaching of the kingdom, the joy of God's presence often challenges our previous assumptions about the way the world works. An example of this dynamic is the parable of the Good Samaritan (Luke 10:29-37). We all know the story. A man is robbed and left for dead on the road between Jerusalem and Jericho. A priest and a Levite walk by, crossing over to the other side of the road. But a Samaritan comes along, reacts with pity, binds the man's wounds, and takes him to an inn, promising to pay for any care he requires.

To get the point of this parable, we have to pay attention to the details. A priest and Levite pass by "on the opposite side" of the road—a road that leads "from Jerusalem to Jericho." Why were these two men on this road? And why did they cross to the other side? Likely these two religious professionals were on their way to the temple, the main reason any religious person would be headed to Jerusalem. And likely they crossed to the other side of the road to avoid stepping in the man's blood or coming too close to what might be a corpse. Jewish law was very clear that such contact made one ritually impure, and thus unable to participate in the temple sacrifices. What Jesus seemed to be suggesting here is that these two men allowed religious observance to get in the way of what was really important: helping their neighbor.

But there is more. After the priest and the Levite came the Samaritan—a character who would have evoked extreme prejudice and disgust among Jesus' listeners. In the minds of good Jews in Jesus' day, Samaritans were half-breed heretics. They were a despised minority who claimed to worship the same God as Jews, but distained the temple and the holy city of Jerusalem. Jesus took this despised figure and made him the hero of the story. In your own mind, substitute for the Samaritan the person for whom you hold the deepest contempt—the person you think of as less than human—and you will get a sense of the impact the story was meant to have.

Jesus was saying to his audience (and to us today), "The way *you* think about the world is not the way *God* thinks about the world." We divide the world into religious people and non-religious people, into Jews and Samaritans, into the good and the bad. But God sees things differently. Like his other parables, the parable of the Good Samaritan was meant to disrupt the religious and social assumptions of Jesus' listeners. As the theologian William Loewe argues, the story "pulls the rug out" from under our world. It forces on all of us a question: "Will I allow my world to go up for grabs like this?"[2]

If Jesus' preaching shatters our old worldview, his actions help us move toward a new one. If Jesus described the reign of God in his teaching, he enacted it in the rest of his ministry.

What Jesus Did

Jesus was known as a healer and as someone who could drive out demons. He was also known to associate with the kind of people good Jews were supposed to avoid. These two facts—Jesus' miracles and the company he kept—were central to his ministry.

Jesus' healing miracles are among the most dramatic stories we find in the New Testament. We read of Jesus bringing sight to the blind, commanding the lame to walk, wiping clean the sores of leprosy, and even raising the dead to life. From our modern scientific perspective, these miracles seem unbelievable and astonishing. We are tempted to treat them on their own as spectacular demonstrations of power, clear proof of the divinity of Jesus. But it would be a mistake to separate Jesus' miracles from his message.

According to the gospels, the miracles of Jesus were not primarily a demonstration of his divinity—nor could they be. In the ancient world, miracles were seen as common—remarkable, but not impossible—and done by any number of people. Being able to perform a miracle would prove you had great power. But it would not prove you were God.

Rather than a demonstration of divinity, Jesus' miracles were the positive flip side of his parables. The parables were meant to disrupt the sinful assumptions of Jesus' audience. They were meant to "pull the rug out" from under their self-centered and skewed views of the world—pointing out what God's reign is *not* like. The miracles were a glimpse into what God's reign *is* like. If the kingdom of God is in fact God's special presence in the world making all things new, then those who were healed by Jesus were the first to taste what that world would be like when the kingdom arrives in all its glory. The miracles were a symbol of hope, a promise of all that is to come. Thus they represented an embodiment of the "already" and "not yet" nature of the kingdom of God, a foretaste of that time when sickness will be no more and death will be destroyed.

The same could be said of Jesus' welcoming of sinners. One of the most distinctive features of Jesus' ministry was his inclusive table fellowship. It seems Jesus would eat with just about anybody. In a world in which social hierarchies and religious boundaries were defined by one's place at the table, Jesus' practice was a cause for real scandal. His enemies called him "a glutton and a drunkard" (Matt 11:19). Religious leaders criticized him for dining with tax collectors and other notorious sinners, people who were ritually unclean and thus a source of defilement to those around them. Women—also a source of uncleanness and temptation—were among Jesus' closest followers, as were the poor, and countless others marginalized by society.

In choosing to break bread with such people, Jesus not only accepted them as full human beings, he also symbolically enacted his vision of the reign of God. This is what the kingdom looks like, Jesus was saying. All of the walls we build up between people, all of the ways we categorize and condemn one another— all of this fades away in the great banquet that is the reign of God. By dining with those the world says he should avoid, Jesus celebrated the beginning of the kingdom. He offered a positive vision of what his mission was all about. Thus his deeds were as much a proclamation of the kingdom of God as were his words. He was demonstrating God's overwhelming love for all.

The radical reversal that Jesus' vision of the reign of God entailed was indeed good news for those ground down by the way the world works—the poor, the marginalized, the socially, economically, and religiously oppressed. But it threatened those who benefitted from the way things were. "The last shall be first" has never been a message readily welcomed by "the first." And so Jesus' words and deeds met resistance. They led to his death. And his ministry cannot be fully understood apart from the way it ended.

How Jesus Died

During a recent RCIA session at our parish, one of the men preparing for baptism announced rather formally, "There is so much that I have gotten out of this process, so much I find beautiful and true about Christianity. But there is one thing I just don't get: Why did Jesus have to die like he did? It seems so pointless. It just doesn't make any sense."

The question was a serious one. And the group fell silent. Our pastor later confessed that, in that moment, a thousand theological explanations ran through his head. But none seemed adequate. None seemed able to respond to the depth of the question. And he too fell silent.

Finally, the oldest member of the group spoke up, "I think Jesus died to show us a different way."

She continued, "In the face of so much evil and suffering in the world, Jesus chose not to fight back or run away. That's what we would do. Instead he chose to face it freely. He stayed true to what he was all about."

Jesus' whole story—his life, death, and resurrection—was about showing us a different way. Sometimes Christians fall into the trap of talking about the death of Jesus as an isolated event. It gets separated out from his life and explained on its own. Jesus *had* to die, the explanation goes. He had to die in order to right our wrongs, to make up for our sins, to pay the penalty for our offenses, to overcome Satan, to open the gates of heaven. His death was a sacrifice to God for us.

Each of these answers contains some truth. But each can also be taken to extremes. And each is always in danger of forgetting the larger context of Jesus' whole story. Jesus proclaimed God's loving presence (the reign of God) in the world. He acted in a way that showed this presence was real. People are more important than religious rules. The poor are filled and the rich go away empty. The last shall be first and the first shall be last. This was not a message that the religious and political elites of his day wanted to hear. In his radical way of loving, Jesus challenged the status quo. He threatened the establishment. And it got him killed.

The crucifixion was not some sadistic torment dreamed up by a bloodthirsty God. It was the natural consequence of the kind of life Jesus lived, in the kind of world in which he lived. His love was risky because it treated as fully human those that the powerful saw as less than human. He lifted up those that "the world" wanted to keep down.

When it became clear that his life and message were becoming dangerous, Jesus did not turn back. In faithfulness to his mission, he continued on to Jerusalem. Entering the temple area, he drove out the money changers. This confrontation with the political, economic, and religious center of power was the last straw. Angered by his actions and concerned about Roman reprisals, a small group of Jewish leaders turned him over to the authorities. Pontius Pilate responded as he would have responded to any threat to Roman authority—with swift and violent force. Jesus was publicly executed as an enemy of the state, hung on a cross in order to show people what happens to those who challenge the powers that be.

In a world of sin, when you love as radically as Jesus loved, you will suffer for it. Jesus knew this, and yet chose to love. The most important thing about Jesus' death is that he faced it freely. He could have run away. He could have toned things down. Instead he stayed faithful to his mission. He lived his life of love *to the end*.

But his death was not the end. On the third day, the women who knew him so well discovered that his tomb was empty. Soon Jesus appeared to his friends. They experienced him as alive. He is risen!

The resurrection was a vindication of Jesus' life of love. It revealed the paschal mystery (from the Hebrew *Pesah* or "Passover," God's deliverance of Israel from Egypt, a salvation that Christians see fulfilled in Jesus). The paschal mystery refers to the death and resurrection of Jesus. It summarizes the great paradox of our faith: only in death is there life, only in dying to self is there rising with God.

Christianity has always rejected the idea that Jesus appeared to his friends as a mere ghost or a figment of their imagination. The gospels have Jesus inviting others to touch his wounds. He eats fish to prove that he is not a mirage.

But the church also teaches that Jesus' resurrection was not simply a resuscitation. He was not raised from the dead like Lazarus, whose new earthly life was still shadowed by the fact that he would one day die. Jesus did not return to earthly life, to the "good old days" of his ministry. Instead he passed beyond space and time. It is hard to describe this in words. The *Catechism of the Catholic Church* calls the resurrection "an historical event . . . that transcends and surpasses history" (CCC 647). The gospels tell of Jesus coming to the disciples through locked doors. His closest friends did not recognize him at first. He appeared and vanished from their sight.

Throughout these stories of the resurrection appearances is a profound sense of newness. It is Jesus, but he is transformed. New life is not like the old. The poet Genevieve Glen captures something of the incredible truth of the resurrection in the closing lines of her Easter hymn "The Sun Arose in Clouds of Fire." As the women run from the tomb, the joy of a new start bursts forth:

> From night to day, from day to night
> The Word goes out through all the earth,
> Borne by the wise whose cry is light:
> Death, death has died—now all is birth!

Who Jesus Is

The stories of Jesus were all told in the light of the resurrection. Having encountered the risen one, early Christians spoke of the significance of Jesus not only in terms of *what he did*, but also in terms of *who he was*. Jesus was not just a gifted teacher or miracle-worker, he was the very presence of God on earth. But how do you speak of the presence of God in a man without compromising the transcendence of God? And how do you speak of a man as God without denying the very humanity that makes him a man? The root of all subsequent church doctrine about Jesus lies in these fundamental questions.

When Jesus asked his disciples, "'Who do you say that I am?'" (Mark 8:29), they answered in the language of their own Jewish faith: you are the Messiah, the Christ, the Anointed One of God! As Christianity spread across the Mediterranean world of the first century, it had to translate this faith into the language of Greek philosophy. Words like *hypostasis* and *ousia*, *person* and *nature*, entered into the Christian vocabulary.

As Christians tried to articulate the truth of the faith in a more philosophically rigorous way, debates broke out between those who stressed the humanity of Jesus and those who stressed the divinity.

In the early fourth century, these debates became so intense that the emperor had to call a council of bishops in order to resolve the dispute. In response to the teaching of a priest named Arius, who argued that it was logically impossible for Jesus to be both God and human, the Council of Nicaea (325 AD) taught that Jesus was and is *fully* God. We still recite the words of the Creed from the Council of Nicaea every Sunday when we profess that Jesus is "God from God, Light from Light, true God from true God."

But Nicaea did not end the debates. And it was more than a hundred years later that the Council of Chalcedon (451 AD) finally reached a resolution between the two sides. There the church found the language that has since stood the test of time. Jesus is *fully* divine and *fully* human—"one in being with the Father according to the divinity, and one in being with us according to the humanity." Any effort to downplay one or the other, any effort to mix them up or keep them totally apart, any effort to change one into the other or to fuse them together is to stray from the true faith of the church.

One of the most important theological consequences of the Council of Chalcedon—beyond quelling the specific debates surrounding the person of Christ—was the broader claim implied by its teaching, namely, that humanity and divinity exist in a *noncompetitive* relationship. By teaching that Jesus was *fully* human and *fully* divine, the council was in effect saying: This is not a zero-sum game. It is not 50-50. Jesus is 100% human and 100% divine. One does not have to give way to the other. One does not have to lose for the other to win.

In the last chapter we talked about how God and the world are related in just this kind of noncompetitive way. The world is perfectly itself as the world *and at the same time* the world is thoroughly permeated by the presence of God, who sustains it in existence. In Jesus we see the most dramatic and intensive example of this noncompetitive coexistence between the Creator and creation. Indeed, it is precisely through Jesus that we learn that God relates to the world in such a way.

This insight into the noncompetitive relationship between God and humanity shatters some of our usual assumptions about human nature. If Jesus is 100% human, and if Jesus is without sin, then sin cannot be essential to being human. (If sin were essential to being human, then Jesus would be missing something and thus could not be *fully* human.) Granted, sin is always present in our lives. But sin is not who we are. In fact, sin is a departure from who we are. It is a rejection or a refusal of our true nature. To sin is to live a false way of being human, it is to live a false self.

Moreover, if in Jesus Christ, humanity and divinity relate in a noncompetitive way, might this not have implications for how we in our humanity relate to God who is divine?

In asking the question we enter into what is known as the paradox of freedom and faithfulness. Many of us tend to assume that faithfulness to God brings with it all kinds of limitations on our human freedom. Faithfulness means all of these things that *I cannot do*. The more faithful I try to be, the less freedom I have to do what I want.

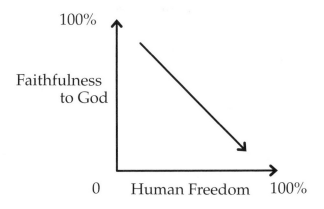

Usual Way of Thinking

Chalcedon helps us to see that faithfulness and freedom are not in fact in competition, but actually go together. To paraphrase the German theologian Karl Rahner: nearness to God and genuine human autonomy grow in direct and not inverse proportion.[3] The image Rahner has in mind comes from those graphs we all learned in math class, with an x-axis running horizontally and a y-axis running vertically. Our usual way of thinking sees freedom decreasing as faithfulness increases; the line runs down (an inverse proportion). What Chalcedon teaches us is that the two increase together; the line runs up (a direct proportion).

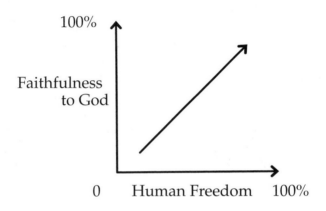

What Chalcedon Teaches

Just as Jesus is fully human and fully divine, so we are most fully free to be ourselves when we are most fully united to God in faithfulness.

An analogy from the experience of human relationships makes this point. I deeply love my wife, Julie. And I consider her presence in my life to be one of God's greatest gifts to me. But I have to admit that when we first started dating, I encountered all of these constraints on my freedom. I wasn't free to dress like a bum or forget to shave. I wasn't free to flirt with other women or spend my Friday nights however I wanted. At the time none of this was a burden, for I was in love with Julie. But our relationship was, without a doubt, a kind of constraint, a diminishment of independence and freedom.

And then we got married! With marriage, a whole host of possible paths in life closed to me. I became no longer free to make major life decisions on my own. I became no longer free to withdraw into my own projects and plans. The same was true for Julie. From one point of view, the more bound together our lives have become, the less freedom each of us has.

But that is just one point of view, and it belies an impoverished notion of freedom. Freedom is not just *freedom from* constraints; it is also *freedom for* a fuller life.

At a deeper level, my relationship with Julie has been one of the most liberating experiences of my life. The more I have grown in love with her, the more I have discovered myself. Our faithfulness to one another has brought incredible freedom—the freedom to open up in honesty without the fear of judgment, the freedom to take risks knowing that you have support, the freedom to admit mistakes and become a better person. Faithfulness and freedom grow in direct and not inverse proportion.

As in our relationships with one another, so in our relationship with God. The closer we are to God, the freer we are to be our true selves. This remains one of the enduring lessons of the Council of Chalcedon.

Theology for Ministry

Jesus was a servant to others. As we have seen in this chapter, his ministry was a life of teaching, healing, and self-sacrifice that revolved around what he called the kingdom of God. This kingdom was good news—the special presence of God bursting into the world, promising to make all that is wrong right. Jesus' vision of God's reign can challenge our assumptions and our prejudices. It can threaten our selfishness and self-centeredness. But at the same time it can be profoundly liberating—drawing us into a freedom that is the path to genuine joy. Jesus' whole life—what he said, what he did, how he died—points toward the joy that comes through serving others.

The first step in developing a Christ-centered ministry is to strive to serve as Jesus served. Clearly we are not talking about a literal imitation of Christ—finding a hill on which to recite the

Sermon on the Mount or commanding the lame to get up and walk. Rather, the effort to serve as Jesus served is a question of grounding whatever we do in the good news of the kingdom of God. Does our ministry challenge the status quo of injustice around us? Does it speak a word of hope to the hopeless? Does it offer love and attention to those who need it most? Does it give some taste of the fellowship that marks the reign of God? Does it provide an "anticipatory experience" of a world transformed? That is what Jesus did. That is what we are called to do. That is the first lesson we learn from the Jesus of the gospels.

We learn a further lesson from later church doctrine about Jesus. And this lesson urges us on to the next step of a Christ-centered ministry. The Council of Chalcedon taught that, in Jesus Christ, humanity and divinity come together in perfect unity. By uniting human nature to God's own self, God raised all human persons to a new dignity. Christians believe that, thanks to the incarnation, Christ has become present within each one of us. And so a deeper ministerial spirituality calls us not just to treat others as Christ would, but to treat others as *Christ*. In other words, we strive not only to *imitate* Jesus, but also to *recognize* him in those we serve.

A student of mine once shared a story about her son Jack. On Jack's tenth birthday, she took Jack and a friend of his out to eat at a favorite restaurant. It was a Chinese place. Jack loved it because he could order extra and then enjoy the leftovers for days.

After dinner, they were all walking out to the car. A homeless man stopped them and asked for a couple of bucks. Without thinking twice, Jack offered the man the Styrofoam container he was carrying, full of his precious leftovers. The man thanked him and went on his way.

Jack's mom was, of course, deeply touched by her son's act of generosity. But she was totally unprepared for what came next.

As she followed the boys into the parking lot, she overheard the friend say to Jack, "Wow, man. That was cool. I bet that sure made Jesus proud."

Jack said to his friend, "Maybe that *was* Jesus."

After my student shared her story with the class, we spent some time talking about the final judgment scene in Matthew

25. We are all familiar with the image. The Son of Man, at the end of time, gathers all the nations before him. He separates the sheep on his right from the goats on his left, welcoming the first into his kingdom and sending the rest to the eternal fire. To those the Son of Man welcomes into his kingdom, he explains, "For I was hungry and you gave me food, I was thirsty and you gave me drink, a stranger and you welcomed me, naked and you clothed me, ill and you cared for me, in prison and you visited me" (Matt 25:35-36).

In their confusion, the sheep ask, "But when did we see you? When did we feed you or clothe you?" And the Son of Man replies, "Whatever you did for the least, you did for me."

In the end, it seems, little else matters.

For Reflection and Discussion

1. Share the images of Jesus you collected at the beginning of the chapter. What attracts you to these images? What do they say about your relationship with Jesus?
2. If you could interview one of the apostles or someone who knew Jesus of Nazareth, what would you most want to know about him? What would be your very first question?
3. "Nearness to God and genuine human autonomy grow in direct and not inverse proportion." If faithfulness and human flourishing grow together, what concrete implications does this have for your ministry?
4. Think of someone that you consider Christlike in her or his ministry? What is it about this person that makes his or her ministry Christlike?

Recommended Reading

United States Catholic Catechism for Adults (Washington, DC: USCCB Publishing, 2006), chapters 7–8.

Catechism of the Catholic Church, second edition (Vatican City: Libreria Editrice Vaticana, 2000), nn. 422–682.

Johnson, Elizabeth A. *Consider Jesus: Waves of Renewal in Christology.* New York: Crossroad, 1992.

Lohfink, Gerhard. *Jesus of Nazareth: What He Wanted, Who He Was.* Collegeville, MN: Liturgical Press, 2012.

Ratzinger, Joseph (Pope Benedict XVI). *Jesus of Nazareth*, 3 vols. New York: Doubleday, 2007–2012.

Rausch, Thomas P. *Who Is Jesus? An Introduction to Christology.* Collegeville, MN: Liturgical Press, 2003.

Senior, Donald. *Jesus: A Gospel Portrait.* Mahwah, NJ: Paulist Press, 1992.

4 In the Spirit . . .

> I have told you this while I am with you. The Advocate, the holy Spirit that the Father will send in my name—he will teach you everything and remind you of all that I told you. (John 14:25-26)

Jesus' time on earth ended with his resurrection and ascension into heaven. But his divine presence remains with us. This presence we call the Holy Spirit.

We Catholics have not always given this topic the attention it deserves. Our Pentecostal brothers and sisters—with their emphasis on charismatic gifts such as healing, prophecy, and speaking in tongues—regularly invoke the power of the Holy Spirit. Eastern Orthodox Christians weave the Holy Spirit seamlessly into their liturgy and theology. But we Roman Catholics too often forget about the third person of the Trinity. The Spirit is not denied, just overlooked—like the friend of a friend brought along to a party, the one guest we never get around to meet.

This neglect is terribly unfortunate, particularly when it comes to ministry. For the Holy Spirit is nothing other than God alive and active in the world today. If Jesus is how God burst forth into human history, then the Spirit is how God continues to burn in the human heart. The Spirit is the way that God reaches out and touches us, drawing us into the divine embrace. And the gifts of the Spirit—the *charisms*—are the way that God turns us around to face the world, ready to serve.

Starting with Experience

It was just a few years ago that I realized something very important about myself: I like to explain things—and I'm pretty good at it!

It sounds conceited to say that out loud, but discerning our gifts for ministry begins with dropping a false modesty that hides what time, experience, and other people keep trying to tell us is true. I like to explain things. I like to order and organize information. But I don't just like to arrange facts, I like to boil things down, discover the core or the essence of an idea, and then articulate it as clearly as I can. I was always attracted to the elegant simplicity of math, and as long as I studied math, I tutored my classmates in it. In graduate school, I avoided the messiness of moral theology and dove into a field of study that I could not have named any better myself: systematic theology. Teaching, studying, writing—these are for me ways of explaining, ways of making sense of a rich and multilayered tradition, ways of inviting others to push deeper, toward the heart of their own experiences, their own convictions, and their own faith.

It took me a while to recognize this aspect of my personality as a gift of the Spirit. "Explaining things" just did not seem to fit what I always assumed a charism to be. But, gradually, I have come to see it as one of the most important ways that the Spirit helps me minister to others.

What are your gifts? What are those aspects of your own personality that, at first glance, seem to have little to do with ministry, but that come into play whenever you relate to others? What are the little things that make you *you*? A sense of humor, a lifelong interest in history or biography, a good ear, a strong back, a critical eye, a green thumb, a drive to ask questions, an ability to remember names or dates, a sense of empathy, a habit of hospitality, a head for numbers, a contrarian streak, a love of sports—nothing is too mundane, too *ordinary*, to be lifted up by the Spirit for service.

Pause and reflect on your own experience. Name your gifts. Identify the Spirit's charisms that shape your personality. If it helps, prepare a ministerial résumé. But instead of listing objectives, education, or past work experience, describe your personal qualities and your strengths as a minister. Reflect on those qualities you have noticed yourself and those that others have pointed out to you. How have your gifts evolved? How have they grown? Note your weaknesses too. Reflect on the role they play in your ministry.

The Spirit of Jesus

This chapter introduces a theology of the Holy Spirit, the source of all charisms for ministry. The Spirit—whose original Hebrew root, *ru'ah*, means "breath" or "wind"—evokes the dynamic and life-giving power of God. "The wind blows where it wills," Jesus told Nicodemus, "you do not know where it comes from or where it goes" (John 3:8). To speak of the Holy Spirit is to speak of God loose in the world—stirring the landscape, whistling through the cracks of our lives, filling our lungs and our sails, carrying us forward.

God is not confined to the stillness of a church. The freedom of God breathes with the Spirit, whom we meet whenever we admire the beauty of God's creation or find forgiveness among friends or act with compassion toward those in need. The Holy Spirit is the active presence of God in the world. The Spirit *is* God, insofar as God continues to move among God's creation. As one theologian put it, whenever we speak of God in a generic way—of our experience of God or of God doing something in our lives—we are speaking of the Spirit.[1]

At the same time, the Holy Spirit is called the third person of the Trinity. But "third person" does not mean "third place"—as if the Spirit always comes last in line. (I have this image in my mind of the Olympics, with a dove standing on the podium wearing a bronze medal.) There is a powerful tendency in our tradition to put the Holy Spirit last, playing a role that comes only *after* the Father creates and the Son saves.

A classic example of this way of thinking can be found in a line from St. Gregory Nazianzus (329–389 AD), who divided all of history into three trinitarian stages:

> The Old Testament proclaimed the Father clearly, but the Son more obscurely. The New Testament revealed the Son and gave us a glimpse of the divinity of the Spirit. Now the Spirit dwells among us and grants us a clearer vision of himself.[2]

If the Old Testament was the time of the Father and the New Testament was the time of the Son, then it is our own time, the time of the church, which is the era of the Holy Spirit. Saint Gregory's words capture something true about the gradual unfolding of God's revelation. But they can easily give the impression that for centuries the Spirit was just sitting around, waiting to get to work. The Bible paints a different picture.

A closer reading of Sacred Scripture reveals the Spirit as present and active from the very beginning. In the book of Genesis, the Spirit (*ru'ah*) hovered over the waters at the moment of creation (Gen 1:2). The Psalms sing of God's Spirit renewing the face of the earth (Ps 104:30). The Book of Wisdom teaches that the Spirit dwells in all things (Wis 12:1). The Spirit purified the sacrifices of the priests, inspired the message of the prophets, and anointed kings to guide the people. This same Spirit, who seems to accompany all of God's activity, continued to work in the life and ministry of Jesus.

The story of Jesus is inseparable from the story of the Spirit. When the angel Gabriel brought the news of new life to Mary, he said, "The holy Spirit will come upon you, and the power of the Most High will overshadow you" (Luke 1:35). Jesus was conceived—as the Creed proclaims—"by the power of the Holy Spirit." The Spirit filled John the Baptist, even from his mother's womb. And when John baptized Jesus in the Jordan River, the Spirit of God descended on Jesus like a dove.

It is the same Spirit who drove Jesus into the desert for forty days and forty nights. Jesus returned "in the power of the Spirit."

At his very first sermon, Jesus proclaimed "The Spirit of the Lord is upon me" (Luke 4:18). Repeatedly the gospels remind us that Jesus' teaching and healing flow out of the Spirit's power.

At every significant moment in the life of Jesus, the Spirit played a role. This was true to the very end. At the Last Supper, Jesus promised his disciples that the Spirit, which in John's gospel he called the "Advocate," would remain with them even after he was gone. This promise was confirmed after the resurrection, when Jesus sent forth his friends by breathing on them and saying, "Receive the holy Spirit" (John 20:22).

In Acts of the Apostles, we find that dramatic scene in which the Holy Spirit descended on the apostles in the form of tongues of fire. These disciples were huddled together in one place, afraid and feeling alone. Suddenly a violent wind rose up, shook the foundation, and filled the entire house. Fire appeared in the air and ignited every person present. Like Jesus, the apostles were filled with the Holy Spirit and began to proclaim the Gospel fearlessly. On fire, Peter stood up before all of Jerusalem and reminded the crowd of the words of the prophet Joel:

> "It will come to pass in the last days," God says,
>   "that I will pour out a portion of my spirit upon all flesh.
> Your sons and your daughters shall prophesy,
>   your young men shall see visions,
>   your old men shall dream dreams." (Acts 2:17)

This Pentecost scene marks the coming of the Spirit and the birth of the church. But as we have seen, it was far from the first entrance of the Holy Spirit into the world. The Spirit cannot be separated from the life of Jesus and the plan of God that goes back to the very beginning of creation.

If the Spirit is the active presence of God in the world and in our lives, then it is hard to put the Spirit last. From the perspective of trinitarian theology, the Spirit comes at the end—proceeding from the Father and the Son. But from the perspective of our experience, the Spirit comes at the beginning. We first feel the movement of God's love in our lives (the Spirit), which then draws us into relationship with Jesus (the Son), who points us beyond to the mystery of God (the Father).[3]

The Gift of God's Love

As we can see, the Bible talks about the activity of the Spirit in a variety of ways. In his own search for a good metaphor to describe the Holy Spirit, Thomas Aquinas suggested that "gift" is especially appropriate. "Gift" is a good image, Aquinas argued, not only because Scripture so often talks about the "gift of the Holy Spirit," but also because of the intimate connection between the giving of a gift and the love that motivates it. As he put it:

> A gift . . . is literally a giving that can have no return, i.e. it is not given with repayment in mind and as such denotes a giving out of good will. Now the basis for such gracious giving is love. . . . And so what we give first to anyone is the love itself with which we love him. Clearly, then, love has the quality of being our first gift; through love we give all other loving gifts.[4]

In any true gift, the first thing that we give to the other is our love. Thus the tradition speaks of the Spirit as the gift of God's love—which is at the same time the gift of God's own self.

There is a wonderful scene from the movie *Dead Poets Society* that illuminates this point. The film tells the story of a group of boys and their teacher at an elite boarding school in the 1950s. In this particular scene, one of the boys, Neil, comes across his roommate in tears. The roommate, Todd, is a shy student, insecure among his friends and overlooked by his family. When Neil asks Todd what is wrong, Todd explains that it is his birthday. He then shows Neil the birthday present he got in the mail from his parents: an expensive leather desk set.

It quickly becomes clear why Todd is upset. The gift is identical to the desk set his parents sent him the year before.

Trying to cheer up his friend, Neil says, "Maybe they thought you needed another one."

Todd replies, "Maybe they weren't thinking about anything at all."

Your heart just breaks for Todd. And it is hard not to be moved by this scene. The desk set symbolizes the chasm between him and his parents. We see that Todd is not hurt by the gift, he is hurt by the relationship. What Todd wants for his birthday is not a *present* from his mom and dad. What he wants is their *presence* in his life. The only gift that really matters is love. And sadly, Todd does not receive this gift from his family.

But he gets it from his friend. The grace of the scene comes as Neil helps Todd hurl the new desk set off the roof. As it crashes to the ground in pieces, Neil comforts Todd with compassion and good humor, "I wouldn't worry. You'll get another one next year."

The gift of the Holy Spirit is not a desk set sent from afar. It is not any *thing* at all. It is the love, the presence, and the friendship of God.

The Charisms of the Spirit

Within the general gift that is the Spirit of God's love are particular gifts of the Spirit that we call *charisms*.

If Catholics of an earlier generation encountered the Spirit in their religious education, it was likely by memorizing lists of the "Gifts of the Holy Spirit" (Wisdom, Understanding, Counsel, Fortitude, Knowledge, Piety, Fear of the Lord) or the "Fruits of the Holy Spirit" (Charity, Joy, Peace, Patience, Kindness, Goodness, Generosity, Gentleness, Faithfulness, Modesty, Self-Control, Chastity). These lists—all based in the Bible, but somewhat arbitrary—were ways for the church to stress the variety of effects the Spirit has on people. They remain ways to recognize when we are being receptive to the movement of God in our lives.

In recent years Catholics have reclaimed another of the Spirit's effects—*charisms*. The word *charism* comes from the simple Greek word for "gift," and it was St. Paul's term for describing those particular gifts of the Holy Spirit given to individuals for the sake of serving others: "There are different kinds of spiritual gifts but the same Spirit; there are different forms of service but the same Lord; there are different workings but the same God who produces all of them in everyone. To each individual the mani- festation of the Spirit is given for some benefit" (1 Cor 12:4-7).

For some benefit. For some help. For some ministry. Char- isms are gifts of the Spirit given to an individual for the good of another. *Serving others* is what separates charisms from all the other gifts and graces and fruits of the Holy Spirit. Medieval theologians distinguished between graces that are given to help a person grow closer to God (*gratia gratum faciens*, "grace mak- ing one graced") and graces given to help a person *help another person* grow closer to God (*gratia gratis data*, "grace gratuitously given"). Charisms fall into this second category.

It bears repeating: charisms help a person *help another person* grow closer to God. We find an eloquent testimony to this no- tion in the words of a woman named Martha, the grandmother of Tessie Prevost.

Tessie Prevost was one of four African-American girls who helped desegregate the New Orleans public school system. In the fall of 1960, Tessie and her classmates—all of six years old— faced the daily ordeal of walking to school through an angry crowd of demonstrators. Federal marshals escorted them past the mob, who hurled obscenities, ugly taunts, and death threats at the children.

One morning Tessie seemed particularly worn out. She had been recovering from the flu and shyly suggested to her grand- mother that she stay home that day. Martha—a kind of mystic in her own right—said that if she were truly sick, that would be fine. But if Tessie was more discouraged than sick, then that was another matter. She encouraged her granddaughter:

> It's no picnic, child—I know that, Tessie—going to that school.
> Lord Almighty, if I could just go with you, and stop there in front
> of that building, and call all those people to my side, and read to
> them from the Bible, and tell them, remind them, that He's up

there, Jesus, watching over all of us—it don't matter who you are and what your skin color is. . . . But I'll tell you, you're doing them a great favor; you're doing them a service, a big service.[5]

Robert Coles, a psychiatrist working with the children, happened to be present that morning. He later reflected on the power of Martha's words. For her grandmother, Tessie was not a victim. She was "not a mere six-year-old black girl from a poor family with no clout and no connections." Rather, she was "an emissary from on high," one called *to serve and save* the very people who were threatening to kill her. Martha reminded her granddaughter that she was nothing less than a minister of God: "You see, my child, you have to help the good Lord with his world! He puts us here—and He calls us to help Him out."

Coles reported that Tessie stood up confidently, put her dishes in the sink, picked up her books, and marched out the door to school.

The idea that God is trying to do good in the world—*and that we ought to help the good Lord with his world*—cuts to the heart of Paul's notion of charism. God *is* trying to do good in the world. And charisms are God's way of getting it done. Charisms are God's way of ministering to people *through* people—through the talents, courage, and gifts of people like Tessie and Martha.

The History of Charisms

In telling the story of charisms, we get off on the wrong foot if we start with the odd and the exciting. It is true that Paul described a wild array of supernatural powers in the early church—prophecy, working of miracles, speaking in tongues, healings, and the discernment of spirits—and he called them all *charisms*. But it is also true that he was always pushing the conversation toward more ordinary experiences and the practical contributions that charisms were meant to make.

For Paul, just because a particular gift is unusual or dramatic does not make it more important than other gifts. In fact, the value of a charism lay not in its power to dazzle, but in its ability to build up the community. Someone might be able to speak in tongues, but if no one could understand the words, then what was the point? If a charism was not used to serve others, then what good was it? Paul seemed to prefer the more ordinary charisms, like teaching and preaching, because they so clearly proclaimed Christ and built up his body, the church.

Charisms are rooted in baptism, broadly available, and oriented toward ministry. In Paul's view, charisms were how God usually worked in the community. No individual or group held a monopoly. Charisms extended to every one of the baptized. Everybody had a piece of the wisdom. Everybody had a gift to share. Paul brought this point home with his famous analogy of the body (1 Cor 12:12-27). Just as a body has many parts, so too the church. And just as in the body every member (even the less honorable parts of the body) has a function, so every member of *Christ's* body, the church, has a role to play. Widespread and ordinary, an expected feature of communal life, charisms find their source in the Holy Spirit and their goal in ministry.

Unfortunately, Paul's vision of broadly available charisms did not last. Over time, charisms moved from the center of church life to the margins of ministry. As Christianity became more and more institutionalized, the free movement of the Spirit seemed unpredictable, difficult to control, even dangerous. The divisions and factions that so worried Paul in Corinth also worried later church leaders. But whereas Paul maintained that every

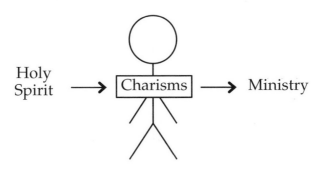

good ministry is based in the Spirit's gifts, later leaders separated important church offices from the charisms. Theologians described charisms as extraordinary graces that come and go. Charisms were real, but not as important as the sacramental ministry of the priest.

None of these observations is meant to ignore the important responsibilities of church leaders who, from the beginning, have been charged not "to extinguish the Spirit, but to test all things and hold fast to what is good" (*Lumen Gentium* 12, quoting 1 Thess 5:19-21). Nor do I mean to suggest that charisms disappeared entirely from the church. Indeed, one of the places the charisms carried on was in the lives of the saints. Here the gifts of the Spirit filled extraordinary individuals, who became models of discipleship and catalysts of ministry.

Father Robert Barron likens the saints to shards of glass—thousands of prisms that refract the one absolutely intense white light of God. Each reflects a particular color and shade along the spectrum of holiness. Together they shine forth in an iridescent explosion. Thus the beauty of the saints is, in part, their variety.[6] It is amazing that there can be so many *different* ways of loving and serving God. To quote C. S. Lewis, "How monotonously alike all the great tyrants and conquerors have been: how gloriously different are the saints."[7]

For centuries, the exemplar of charism was the saint—a heroic Christian whose special gifts were evident to all and who stood as living proof of the Spirit's ongoing activity in the church. When the saint was also the founder of a religious order, we would say that these gifts were passed on to those who followed in her or his footsteps, shaping the "charism" of the order.

If the gain here is evident, perhaps too is the loss. The emphasis on saints tended to limit the idea of charism to the extraordinary or the exceptional. It tended to restrict it to a small group or to special individuals. In many ways, this understanding repeated some of the same misunderstandings that Paul fought so hard to correct. And if, in our own day, we have reclaimed a broader and more inclusive notion of charism, then it is only because we have come to see what Paul always knew: Charisms are what empower *all* Christians to do ordinary things extraordinarily well.

Vatican II on Charisms

The Second Vatican Council was the real catalyst for recovering Paul's vision of charisms. But there was plenty of resistance along the way. Some of the bishops at Vatican II clung to the assumption that charisms could only be fantastic and few. They wanted to limit these gifts to the extraordinary and miraculous manifestations of the Spirit. Others argued that charisms are more ordinary and widespread. Cardinal Leo Josef Suenens presented this position in the form of a question:

> Do we not all know laymen and laywomen in each of our own dioceses who we might say are in a way called by the Lord and endowed with various charisms of the Spirit? Whether in catechetical work, in spreading the Gospel, in every area of Catholic activity in social and charitable works? . . . Charisms in the Church without the ministry of pastors would certainly be disorderly, but vice versa, ecclesiastical ministry without charisms would be poor and sterile.[8]

In the end, this broader view prevailed. The Dogmatic Constitution on the Church acknowledged that the Spirit bestows on the church "different hierarchic and charismatic gifts" which together contribute to the church's life and mission (*Lumen Gentium* 4). Later on, the document offered a fuller description of these gifts:

> Moreover, it is not only through the sacraments and the ministries that the holy Spirit makes the people holy, leads them and enriches them with his virtues. Allotting his gifts "at will to each individual," he also distributes special graces among the faithful of every rank. By these gifts, he makes them fit and ready to undertake various tasks and offices for the renewal and building up of the church, as it is written, "the manifestation of the

Spirit is given to everyone for profit." Whether these charisms be very remarkable or more simple and widely diffused, they are to be received with thanksgiving and consolation since they are primarily suited to and useful for the needs of the church. (*Lumen Gentium* 12)

As this passage makes clear, charisms flow out of the Spirit and flow into some kind of service within and on behalf of the church. Less charisms appear too "churchy" or inward-looking, the council's Decree on the Apostolate of Lay People explained that charisms also have an orientation toward the larger world: "From the reception of these charisms, even the most ordinary ones, there follow for all Christian believers the right and duty to use them in the church and in the world for the good of humanity and the development of the church" (*Apostolicam Actuositatem* 3).

Discerning Our Gifts

If charisms are gifts of the Spirit given for the good of ministry, then the discernment of charisms is not a luxury for lay ministers. Indeed, this discernment is at the heart of the call to serve.

The task of discernment involves the process of coming to know and accept one's gifts. It is as simple—and as difficult—as coming to know and accept oneself. Father John Haughey admits that charisms are notoriously elusive. Trying to pin them down is like trying "to bottle wind or package fire," because they take as many forms as there are individuals receiving them.[9] But he suggests a fruitful starting point for discernment in the old adage: grace builds on nature.

To understand what God is calling me to do, I begin by asking who God created me to be.

What is the relationship between supernatural charisms and our own natural talents and abilities? The Catholic conviction that "grace builds on nature" warns against separating the two too much. The Spirit's charisms are not magical powers that transform introverts into extroverts or disorganized volunteers into master administrators. Rather, the grace of the Spirit builds on our own natural interests and the skills we cultivate. "A charism is often a power God's Spirit imbues human beings with that enables them to do better what nature or training or praxis has first equipped them to do, thus enhancing what is already there."[10]

If some Protestant traditions have stressed the fallenness of creation and the sinfulness of humanity, the Catholic tradition has tended to see more harmony between nature (creation, our own human-ness) and grace (salvation, the supernatural presence of God in our lives). There is a continuity between who God created me to be and who God calls me to become. Charisms cannot be an arbitrary "add-on" to our personality, because our personality is already graced by these spiritual gifts from the beginning. They help me to serve in the unique way that God built me to serve.

If I were to offer an analogy for the relationship between charism and personality—between supernatural gift and natural ability—I would say that charisms are like the love of a parent that encourages a child's innate talents. The Spirit is, after all, the love of God, and charisms are a facet of that love. At the moment of my conception, God created me as a perfectly unique person, and from that moment God has loved everything about me. (Keep in mind that my sins are not me, they are actually a turning away from myself—the true self that God made me to be.)

In loving me, God also loves those particular dimensions of my personality that I use to serve others (such as my openness to new experiences, my empathy, or my sense of humor). By loving these aspects of my personality, God encourages them, enhances them, and so helps me use them more effectively to serve the reign of God. What is a charism? *A charism is God's love for what I do to help others, a love that helps me do it more beautifully.*

As we move through the process of discernment, we start to see that some aspects of our personalities are more central than others, some are more obviously geared toward ministry than others. Moreover, they impact our lives differently. Haughey distinguishes between charisms that are *role-enhancing* and charisms that are *life-consuming.* Both are important in the life of the church, but they lead to different effects in the life of an individual. Role-enhancing charisms are gifts that help us do particular ministries particularly well. Life-consuming charisms are those gifts that "sear into the deepest marrow of a person" orienting that person's whole life toward service.[11] The charism of prophecy that infuses the lives of the Old Testament prophets serves as a classic example. But we may know people in our own lives who are just as carried away by such a life-orienting call. Who knows, you may be one of them! For most of us, however, it is the more modest gifts—like the ability to explain things clearly—that represent the promptings of the Spirit toward service. These gifts are often so hidden and so humble that they can be easily missed. Discernment, then, is about developing an ear to hear. It is listening for a voice that is not far off, but very, very close, welling up from within.

Finally, since charisms flow from the Spirit through our created personality, they follow natural patterns of growth and development. They are not static. They change. Some gifts develop as we are called to respond to new needs. Some fade as we move out of old ministries or fail to nurture them. It is a question of potential. Am I ready for what I am being asked to do now? If further training is needed, am I open to it? Will this ministry allow me to continue to grow and expand? Charisms "take time," Haughey explains, "and attention and cultivation and desire and encouragement and perseverance and exercise." But if we fail to cultivate our gifts for others, then it is hard to see "how they would ever grow into effectiveness."[12]

Gifts Given for Others

Therein lies the key: since charisms are given to me for the good of another, they are not my personal possession. I cannot hoard them or selfishly claim them as *mine*. To do so would be like the child who hides a pint of ice cream in her room so that she doesn't have to share, only to find it all melted away at the end of the day. My gifts are part of me in the most intimate way possible, but I do not own them. They survive as part of me only insofar as I give them away to someone else. They are, after all, a gift, and as Jesus reminded his followers, what you receive as a gift, you are to give as a gift (Matt 10:8).

How might my particular gifts help the people around me? How might they serve the church and the world? As we have seen, what sets charisms apart from other gifts and graces of God is that charisms are graces given to one person for the good of another. When Paul asked, "What good is it for someone to speak in tongues if there is no one to interpret?" he was cutting to the heart of what charisms are all about. Better to speak five words in plain English or simple Spanish than to speak ten thousand words in a tongue that nobody can understand (1 Cor 14:19).

Charisms are, by definition, oriented toward needs in the community. Thus the process of discernment will require at least as much attention to those around me as it requires attention to myself. And the Spirit celebrates when these two come together. Frederick Buechner captured this insight perfectly when he described a calling as the place where my "deep gladness and the world's deep hunger meet."[13] There is no question that the world needs us. Suffering is great. The hunger is real. We might be tempted to turn away from our neighbors in need. But to do so, to close in on oneself, to fail to love, is to transform what is beautiful into something dull, even ugly. It is to become "a resounding gong or a clashing cymbal" (1 Cor 13:1), rather than God's instrument, contributing its own distinct music to the symphony of the Spirit.

Theology for Ministry

The theology of charisms laid out in this chapter encourages us to spend some time coming to know our individual gifts and our personal strengths. Good and faithful ministry emerges out of harmony, not discord. What we want to hear are resonances between who we are and how we serve.

At the same time, we should not ignore our weaknesses. They teach us as much about ourselves as do our strengths.

Never would we want to deny the potential for growth, or deny the truth that God—at times—might be calling us beyond our comfort zone. Still, to affirm the need for growth is not to imply that we have to overcome every one of our limitations. Limitations can be our friends, and we ought to welcome them. In a culture that believes "anyone can achieve anything," this is a tough sell. But it is crucial. The great Protestant theologian Karl Barth argued that accepting our limitations is a key step in vocational discernment, because our limitations are one of the most important ways God reveals our callings to us.[14] I will never be a concert pianist. To say so is not a failure of nerve or a cowardly "giving up." It is a recognition of reality! And it does not make me sad. It would only be sad if I failed to see it.

In thinking about our own ministerial lives and the difficult honesty that discernment demands, we should take some comfort in the words of a prayer crafted by Bishop Ken Untener, a prayer that later came to be called "The Romero Prayer." It includes the following insight: "We cannot do everything, and there is a sense of liberation in realizing that. This enables us to do something, and to do it very well."[15] The recognition that I cannot do *everything* frees me to do *something*—to love God and others in a way that only I can.

If Jesus calls us to give ourselves away, we can only give *ourselves* away. That is what ministerial charisms are all about. I cannot give someone else away. *I* can only give *me*.

Michael Himes once described the fifteenth-century classic *The Imitation of Christ*, by Thomas à Kempis, as having the most dangerously misleading title in the history of Christian spirituality. We have all heard the notion that we should strive to imitate Christ ("What would Jesus do?") or that we should strive to imitate the saints. But for Himes, while there is much to learn from these heroes of holiness, we should not look to the saints—not even to Jesus—for an exact pattern to copy. Instead, we should look to these holy women and men for *encouragement* to discover our own unique pattern of serving others. "God has already given the world a Francis of Assisi. It does not need a second."[16]

Sadly, most of us in ministry, at one point or another, try to be Francis of Assisi. We try to be the "ideal" minister. And the result is burnout. It is common to assume that burnout comes from trying to give too much. But as the writer Parker Palmer suggests, burnout is not about giving too much, it's about giving too little. It's about trying to give what we do not have. Burnout follows when we try (or are forced) over an extended period of time to do what we are not very good at, to serve in ways we are ill-equipped to serve, to work without the joy of genuine self-gift or with no avenues to share our strengths. "Burnout is a state of emptiness, to be sure, but it does not result from giving all I have: it merely reveals the nothingness from which I was trying to give in the first place."[17] It is like trying to give someone *else* away, day after day.

Healthy ministry flows out of genuine charisms—honestly recognized and generously shared. Such a response to the Spirit's gifts, whether through lifelong, full-time ministry or through more occasional acts of service, ought to be a source of joy—not necessarily happiness or ease, but *joy*, a deep consolation that carries one through all the craziness and conflict, all the disagreements and disappointments. It brings with it the simple delight of knowing that God is simply delighting in our response, rooting us on, "Yes! That's what I made you for!" I think of those arresting words from the end of the movie *Chariots of Fire*. As Eric Liddell, the devout Christian whose religious convictions lie at the heart of the film, sprints toward the finish line, we hear his voice articulate a deep theology of charism: "I believe God made me for a purpose. But he also made me *fast* . . . and when I run, I feel his pleasure."

For all the reality of our limitations, for all the danger of burnout, the biggest challenge remains igniting genuine charisms rather than extinguishing them. It can be hard to admit how fast we can run. It can be even harder to accept that God enjoys it when we do. It is true that many people have an overinflated sense of themselves. This is as much a problem in church ministry as it is in any other realm of life. But in my experience, the greater risk comes not from people who think they have gifts they do not have, but rather from people who do not recognize the gifts they do have.

For Reflection and Discussion

1. Share the ministerial résumé you compiled earlier in the chapter. Were you surprised by any of the personal qualities you listed? What do you see as your greatest strengths? Are you using the gifts that you have been given?
2. The next time you are at Mass, pay attention to every time the Holy Spirit is mentioned. What do these references to the Spirit suggest? What is the image of the Holy Spirit that emerges from our liturgy?
3. Reflect on your own gifts for ministry. Are these gifts "role-enhancing" or "life-consuming"? How so? Reflect on your own history in ministry. How have you seen your gifts develop and grow?
4. Describe an experience where you felt God communicating to you in and through your limitations. How was God calling you?

Recommended Reading

United States Catholic Catechism for Adults (Washington, DC: USCCB Publishing, 2006), chapter 9.

Catechism of the Catholic Church, second edition (Vatican City: Libreria Editrice Vaticana, 2000), nn. 683–747.

Cordes, Paul Josef. *Call to Holiness: Reflections on the Catholic Charismatic Renewal.* Collegeville, MN: Liturgical Press, 1997.

Donnelly, Doris, ed. *Retrieving Charisms for the Twenty-First Century.* Collegeville, MN: Liturgical Press, 1999.

Dougherty, Rose Mary. *Discernment: A Path to Spiritual Awakening.* Mahwah, NJ: Paulist Press, 2009.

Goergen, Donald J. *Fire of Love: Encountering the Holy Spirit.* Mahwah, NJ: Paulist Press, 2006.

O'Meara, Thomas F. *Theology of Ministry.* Revised Ed. Mahwah, NJ: Paulist Press, 1999.

5 With Others . . .

When Jesus returned to Capernaum after some days, it became known that he was at home. Many gathered together so that there was no longer room for them, not even around the door, and he preached the word to them. They came bringing to him a paralytic carried by four men. Unable to get near Jesus because of the crowd, they opened up the roof above him. After they had broken through, they let down the mat on which the paralytic was lying. (Mark 2:1-4)

I hate crowds. I hate that feeling of being closed in and unable to move. I hate feeling trapped. Traffic jams, congested lines at an amusement park, the bottleneck at the exits leaving a football game—these are for me a little taste of hell, which I imagine as a hot, impossibly-crowded room with one open door that nobody can ever reach.

In this passage from Mark's gospel, the paralytic is trapped, but not by other people. It is his body that prevents him from moving. His shriveled legs close him off. They keep him from getting up and going to see this new prophet who has come to Capernaum.

If his body closes things off, then it is this man's friends who open things up. For the paralytic, other people are not hell, they are heaven!

Think about the friends who carry this man to Christ. Whose idea was it to take him to Jesus? Who came up with the plan to go through the roof? What kind of faith and love for their friend drove these people to do what they did? Would I have been so determined? Seeing the crowd, I might have said, "Let's come back later, when Jesus is not so busy." But these guys were unstoppable! They would not give up until they got to Jesus. Can you imagine the thrill when they looked down though that roof and saw their friend stand up?

Starting with Experience

As infants, our parents brought us up to the baptismal font. They literally carried us to Christ. That simple gesture communicates a profound truth: We are raised in a community of faith. We are connected to God through one another.

When our first daughter was baptized, our associate pastor Fr. Neil presided. Father Neil had just returned to the United States after twenty years of missionary work in East Africa. And on Kate's baptism day, he transformed our suburban liturgy into a village celebration.

Father Neil led six sets of parents, godparents, and the entire assembly in an unrehearsed procession around the church. He called everyone out from the pews in order to crowd around the large baptismal font in the gathering space.

Kids elbowed their way up to the water. Parents juggled babies in delicate baptismal gowns and jostled for a place near the front. Godparents burned themselves on candle wax while grandparents strained to get photos. Everyone pressed in to see. Kate was dipped in water and slathered with oil and passed around the congregation. The church erupted in spontaneous applause.

It was a mob scene.

But in this chaos of coming to Christ one thing was clear: Kate was not in this alone.

Pause and reflect on your own experience. Who carried you to Christ? Who are the people who brought you to Jesus? If it helps, close your eyes and imagine yourself in the gospel scene we just read. You are the paralytic, asleep on your mat. All of a sudden, the mat jostles and begins to move. You feel yourself being carried along. You open your eyes and look up. Who do you see smiling down on you? Parents? Teachers? A parish priest? A Cursillo leader? A best friend? A spouse? Who are the ones who, over the course of your life, have brought you to Jesus?

We Go to God Together

In this chapter we explore the communal context within which our faith is lived. We explore the church. But the church is ultimately rooted in our relationships, in our connections to those people who have shaped our relationship with God.

The Catholic tradition is a communal one. As the late Fr. Andrew Greeley once put it, "Catholics cluster, they bond, they converge, they swarm. Catholicism in James Joyce's happy phrase means 'Here comes everybody!'"[1]

In other words, we go to God together.

My first year in college I took a calculus class that was almost the end of me. (It was definitely the end of my plans to major in math.) In order to survive, I joined a study group of about a half-dozen students who met every week to work on the homework and to offer what we could of moral support.

One of the benefits of this study group was that I got to know (and then developed a crush on) a classmate named Elizabeth. I enjoyed getting to know her. And calculus didn't seem so bad if I could work on it sitting next to her.

As we came to the end of the year, and the final exam approached, our group planned a marathon study session the night before the test. When I arrived I was surprised to see that Elizabeth was not there. She almost never missed a session, and this was a very important review. I saw her the next morning at the exam, however, and I caught up with her after we finished.

The first thing Elizabeth said was, "I'm pretty sure I just failed that exam."

"Why didn't you come to the review last night?" I asked.

Elizabeth explained that one of her friends was going away to study abroad the next semester. At the last minute, a group of women from her dorm decided to take their friend out to dinner. They spent all night hanging out, sharing stories from freshman year, and sending off their friend. By the time they had finished, it was too late to get to the study session or to prepare for the test.

Surprised by what seemed to me to be a totally irresponsible decision, I blurted out lamely, "How could you do that? The exam was worth 40 percent of the grade!"

Elizabeth looked at me as if I were a lost cause and said, "Ed, people last."

It took me some time to appreciate what Elizabeth meant. She did not say "people come last." She said "people last." People *endure.* People *matter.* Whether she realized it or not, Elizabeth pointed me toward one of the deepest truths of our faith.

I don't remember a single thing from that study session. But I will never forget what Elizabeth taught me with those two words: *People last.*

It is often said, "You can't take it with you." And it is true, there are so many things—our material possessions, our retirement plans, our reputations, our college grades—that we cannot take with us when we die. But there is one thing that we can take: our relationships. That is one of the very few things we are certain will carry over from this life into the next. *People last.*

The Catholic doctrine of the communion of saints affirms that, in heaven, we will not be alone. We will be surrounded by all those "friends of God and prophets" (Wis 7:27) who have touched our lives. We are all tied together—to the very end.

What is the Church?

A few years ago I saw a bumper sticker, written in the recognizable font of the popular television series *Crime Scene Investigation*. It read: "C.S.I.: Christ Saves Individuals."

I thought it was cute, but not quite right. To stress that Christ saves *individuals* overlooks an important conviction that is stated forcefully at the beginning of Vatican II's Dogmatic Constitution on the Church:

> At all times and in every nation, anyone who fears God and does what is right has been acceptable to him. He has, however, willed to make women and men holy and to save them, *not as individuals without any body between them*, but rather to make them *into a people* who might acknowledge him and serve him in holiness. (*Lumen Gentium* 9, emphasis added)

Without a doubt, God touches each of us as unique individuals. But God also draws us together.

The original Greek word for church was *ekklesia*, which gives us "ecclesiology," meaning "the study of the nature and mission of the church." In its original sense, *ekklesia* meant "those called" or "the assembly of those who are called." At its most basic level, the church is the community of people called by Jesus to be his disciples.

This emphasis on call was highlighted by Pope John Paul II when he described the church itself as a "mystery of vocation" (*mysterium vocationis*). The church is a "con-vocation"—a calling together. It comes into being thanks to God's call, and every Christian calling takes place within it. The pope went on to explain: "Each Christian vocation comes from God and is God's gift. However, it is never bestowed outside of or independently of the church. Instead it always comes about in the church and through the church."[2]

Today we use the word "church" in a variety of ways. It can describe a *building* ("We need to fix the church roof") or a *worship service* ("We're going to church"). It can indicate a specific *denomination* ("the United Methodist Church") or the *universal body* of those who are baptized into Christ. In can refer to the *hierarchy* in Rome ("What does the church teach?") or one's local *parish* ("We just love our church"). In this chapter, I use the word "church" primarily in reference to the Roman Catholic Church. And by it I mean to describe the whole body of believers—clergy and laity alike—who are called together by baptism to enter into communion with God and with one another, and who are sent out to serve the reign of God in the world.

Jesus and the Church

All Christians trace the church back to Jesus. But they have not always agreed on just exactly how we got from Jesus to the church. To simplify a complicated debate, we might say that Catholics have tended to emphasize *continuity* between Jesus and the church structures that followed. Protestants have tended to emphasize *discontinuity*.

Catholic theologians once argued that, during his earthly life, Jesus laid out in precise detail the shape of all later church institutions. In their eyes, Jesus "founded" the church in the sense that he *designed a structure*. They tried to show how Jesus established the seven sacraments, specified a comprehensive moral code, assigned a pope to lead the universal church, and set up bishops and priests to assist. In its most extreme forms, this view gave the impression that Jesus left behind a master blueprint that spelled out everything from the number of holy days to the color of the popemobile!

Protestants, on the other hand, used to argue that Jesus was not so concerned about structures. Instead, Jesus simply *inspired a community* of people with his message. Jesus had little interest in externals, he gave little thought to what would come after him. Rather, he offered an inspirational message and then left it up to his followers to create their own institutions, ministerial roles, and hierarchies. In its most extreme forms, this view gave the impression that Jesus would be surprised (and not a little disappointed) to see what his followers had come up with!

In the context of post-Reformation debates, these two views hardened. Catholics, who wanted to defend the many structures that Protestants were challenging (such as the papacy, priesthood, and the sacraments), argued that these structures had to go all the way back to Jesus. Protestants called for more freedom to reform these structures. Thus they argued that many of them were human creations that could be changed. Catholics tended to be top-down: Christ gives all authority to the hierarchy, who then create the community. Protestants tended to be bottom-up: Christ gives all authority to the community, which then creates the ministries it needs.

In part as a result of Vatican II, Catholics and Protestants began to talk to one another in more constructive ways. And out of that dialogue came a more nuanced understanding. Without the bias of past debates blinding them, both sides began to see what contemporary biblical scholarship was beginning to uncover.

That scholarship reveals that Jesus did not seem particularly preoccupied with setting up a hierarchy. But he was not indifferent to the movement he had begun. Jesus was focused on his mission. But he also did certain things to ensure that his mission would go on. He gathered disciples and commissioned them to preach. He began certain practices (such as teaching, healing, and sharing a meal) that he expected would continue ("Do this in memory of me"). He appointed the Twelve to symbolize a new Israel and gave Peter a central role.

Today almost everyone agrees that the relationship between Jesus and the church is neither pure continuity nor pure discontinuity, but rather *development*—which involves a kind of "discontinuity within continuity." We should not play structure off of community, as if the two were mutually exclusive. From the beginning, the church was not *just* a structure or *just* a community. The church was, and remains, a *structured community*, an ordered communion.

Early Churches

To say that the church was a structured community from the start is not to suggest that it was a monolith. In fact, the New

Testament reveals that the early Christian communities were quite diverse.

In *The Churches the Apostles Left Behind*, the noted biblical scholar Fr. Raymond Brown identified at least seven different "types" of Christian communities in the first century. He described the considerable variety among these churches in terms of their self-understanding, makeup, and ministerial structures. While they all shared a common commitment to the saving message of Jesus Christ, there was no single mold into which they all fit.

We have to keep in mind that, at the beginning, Christianity was a relatively small religious movement. The sociologist Rodney Stark estimates that by the year 40 AD there were only about 1,000 Christians in the world. Ten years later, there were about 1,400, and by the year 100 there were approximately 7,530.[3] These numbers represent a healthy rate of growth. Still, by the end of the first century, Christians represented less than 0.02% of the population of the Roman Empire. Seventy years after the resurrection of Jesus, you could fit all of the Christians in the world into two of today's average-sized suburban parishes.

So when we think of "the church" at the beginning, we have to imagine tiny communities scattered around the Mediterranean, communities made up of anywhere from twenty or thirty to sixty or seventy members, gathering in homes, celebrating simple rituals, with only the most basic administrative structures.

Like small parishes today, each of these Christian communities was unique. Each was a reflection of its own particular history (Who "founded" their group? What crises had they faced?), location (City or rural?), and make-up (Jew, Gentile, or somewhere in between?). The differences emerged out of the diversity of situations, challenges, and responses that marked each particular community.

A good example of this diversity is the canonical collection of gospels themselves, each of which paints a distinctive portrait of Jesus (crafts a distinctive *mosaic*) precisely because each emerged out of a different community of Christians. Daniel Harrington summarizes this nicely: "While some (Mark's community) faced persecution from the Roman authorities, others (Matthew's community) felt the need to define themselves with respect to their Jewish roots and rivals; still others (Luke's community) sought to find their place in salvation history and in the world of the Roman Empire."[4]

Given their different contexts and concerns, what is remarkable is that these communities found ways to stay connected. First and foremost, they prayed for one another. As a symbol of spiritual solidarity, some churches would even send consecrated bread from their Eucharist to other churches in the area. These churches would also exchange letters. As time went on, church leaders would occasionally gather together in meetings, or synods. Communities would invite neighboring bishops to join in the consecration of a new bishop. And the bishop of Rome gradually took on more and more responsibility for guiding and coordinating these many local communities.

Church through the Ages

One way to tell the story of the church from the New Testament to the present is to tell the story of *church buildings*. Architecture and art often give us clues into the different ways that ancient communities understood themselves, organized their life, and served others. They give us a window into the past.[5]

It is an interesting fact that the earliest Christians did not build temples. In the ancient world, religion revolved around temples—whether the many pagan temples that dotted the landscape or the one Jewish temple that dominated Jerusalem. Christians did not build temples for their community because, in their minds, *the community was the temple*. They saw themselves as living stones, built into a sanctuary with Jesus as the cornerstone (1 Pet 2:4-5). When Christians first began to gather, they gathered in one another's homes. They formed *house churches*. There they remembered the stories of Jesus, baptized new members, sang hymns, and broke bread. The experience of church was "homey," informal, flexible, and broadly participative.

A lot of things had changed by the year 313 AD, when the Emperor Constantine threw his allegiance to Jesus and issued a formal declaration of toleration for all Christians. By the end of that century, Christianity had become the official religion of the Roman Empire. These events transformed Christianity from a suspicious movement on the margins of society into a major cultural force. As people flooded into the church, leadership roles, doctrines, and rituals became increasingly formalized. Everything became more "official." When they needed more space to accommodate all these new members, Christians still did not build temples. Instead, they adopted a secular model, the *basilica*, the "hall of the king."

The basilica was a long rectangular building (the nave) with a semi-circular addition on one end (the apse). It was a simple, functional building—designed by the Romans to allow the emperor, governor, or other official, seated in the apse, to be seen and heard by people in the nave. When Christians moved their Sunday worship into the basilicas, the nature of the celebration changed. Liturgy became more formal and more scripted, with elaborate processions and clear distinctions among ministers. These shifts reflected what was going on in the community, as church leaders began to adopt many of the trappings of imperial

Early Basilica

power. The bishop sat in the apse, exactly where the Roman governor used to sit. And the people—the new "citizens" of the church—remained in the nave. This separation between the apse and the nave symbolized the growing separation between the clergy (who saw themselves as benevolent rulers) and the laity (who saw themselves as obedient subjects).

Centuries of decline followed the fall of the Roman Empire in the fourth century. But by the twelfth and thirteenth centuries, new life was breathing through medieval Europe. A series of engineering innovations and artistic breakthroughs culminated in what many consider to be the pinnacle of church architecture, the gothic *cathedral*. It is hard to summarize the complexity and symbolism of a gothic cathedral. But to walk into the cathedrals of Chartres or Notre Dame is to be drawn up and out into the transcendent beauty of heaven itself. Stone arches let the ceilings soar, external supports (flying buttresses) open up space in the thick walls for stained glass, elaborate carvings arrange all of creation—from angels to ants—into a cohesive whole.

Medieval people loved order. They would organize thousands of pieces of colored glass into a window that told a single story. They would position hundreds of statues on the face of a cathedral to show the design of the universe. Everything had its place appointed by God. *Hierarchy* (literally, "sacred order") was the great ideal—a view of all of reality arranged in a kind of ladder, with God at the top.

The church applied this ideal of hierarchy to its own life. Everything and everyone had a divinely-appointed place. The circle of disciples gathered around the Lord's table became a giant pyramid with the pope on top, followed by his cardinals and archbishops, bishops and priests, religious and other ministers. At the bottom of the pyramid were the laity. They became passive recipients of the ministry of the ordained.

As history moved from the Middle Ages into the early modern period, the church passed through the Protestant Reformation and the Catholic Counter-Reformation into a new era of vitality. Thomas O'Meara calls this new period "Baroque Catholicism." And *baroque churches* capture something of the energy of God at work in the world. Angels burst onto the scene, marble seems to move. Light floods down to illuminate statues of saints in dynamic poses, superheroes of Catholic holiness. In their lesser forms, baroque churches appear overdone, even gaudy. But in their best examples, they give a glimpse of a church waking up to a world-wide and dynamic mission.

In the most famous of these baroque churches, St. Peter's Basilica in Rome, we see what the church of this time thought of itself. Built on top of the tomb of St. Peter, this baroque basilica stands as a multimedia celebration of his successor, the pope. Every element of the church turns our attention to the papacy— the huge bronze canopy over the tomb, the throne of Peter, the dove of inspiration breaking through the far window, the words "Feed my sheep" etched under the dome. Following the Reformation, it would be the pope who would hold together what remained of the Catholic Church. Following Columbus, it would be the pope who would direct a new missionary impulse. The colonnade of pillars that surround St. Peter's Square are like the arms of the church reaching out to gather in the whole world.

Today we recognize the tragic legacy of conquest, contamination, and colonization that came with this universal mission. The arms extended out to the "New World" were also arms that stole, enslaved, and killed the native peoples "discovered" there. In our own day, we mourn the way in which European Christians destroyed whole civilizations and devastated whole continents. But, at that time, it all seemed to be the will of God. Missionaries saw themselves saving the souls of heathens—leaving behind a legacy of evangelization hidden today, right before our eyes, in all the cities—from San Francisco to San Antonio to Sao Paulo—named after saints. But the fact that so few Christians spoke out against the evils of the age is itself a window into the church of that era.

As Europe entered into the Age of Enlightenment in the seventeenth and eighteenth centuries, the Catholic Church began its long retreat from the modern world. Threatened by modern philosophies and scientific discoveries that seemed to threaten church authority and biblical truths, Catholics looked back to an earlier Golden Age for comfort. They build neo-Gothic churches and read medieval theologians. European immigrants to the United States wanted church buildings that looked like what they left behind in the Old Country. They kept the devotions and prayers their parents had taught them. The nineteenth and early twentieth century was a period of *Romanticism* in church architecture and in church life. The church deliberately cut itself off from the surrounding culture, hoping to sustain the faith in a safer womb.

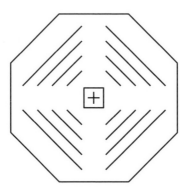

Contemporary Church

By the middle of the twentieth century, Catholics began to build churches in a *modern* style, but with limited success. Even today we still search for the right way to create sacred spaces in modern (and postmodern) forms. However, one of the promising developments over the past fifty years has been the care with which communities are now designing their church buildings with an eye to the liturgies that are celebrated within them. In the prominence given to the baptismal font, in the way in which the seating brings the assembly closer to the presider and to one another, in the focus on the ritual action around the altar, in the noble simplicity of the most important liturgical symbols—in all of these design decisions, we can see something of a new vision of church, a vision proclaimed by the Second Vatican Council.

The Church of the Second Vatican Council

So far we have focused on the external features of the church—the "human side" of the church, if you will. One of the most important contributions of the Second Vatican Council was the reminder that the church has a "divine side" too. The church has a deeper spiritual dimension. The church is, in the words of Pope Paul VI, a mystery, that is, "a reality imbued with the hidden presence of God."

The very first document produced by the council, the Constitution on the Sacred Liturgy, proclaimed this twofold nature of the church:

> For the church is both human and divine, visible but endowed with invisible realities, zealous in action and dedicated to contemplation, present in the world, yet a migrant, so constituted that in it the human is directed toward and subordinated to the divine, the visible to the invisible, action to contemplation, and this present world to that city yet to come, the object of our quest. (*Sacrosanctum Concilium* 2)

Elsewhere, Vatican II compared this twofold nature of the church to a sacrament—traditionally defined as "a visible sign of an invisible reality." Thus, according to the Dogmatic Constitution on the Church, "the church, in Christ, is a sacrament—a sign and instrument, that is, of communion with God and of the unity of the entire human race" (*Lumen Gentium* 1).

If we genuinely believe that the church is "a reality imbued with the hidden presence of God," then we have to admit that no one definition can fully capture the mystery. Vatican II avoids such a definition. Instead it offers a variety of images for the church. Three of these metaphors stand out: the church is the people of God, the Body of Christ, and the temple of the Holy Spirit.

By describing the church as the *people of God*, Vatican II meant to affirm that the church includes all baptized believers—clergy and laity, married and celibate, young and old. "The church" cannot be reduced to the hierarchy. It includes everyone. We are the church!

On this topic, the history of Vatican II's Constitution on the Church is helpful to know. An earlier draft of this document began with a chapter on "The Mystery of the Church." It then moved on to a chapter on the hierarchy, followed by a chapter on the laity and a chapter on religious. In discussing this draft, the bishops decided they needed a new chapter—one on "the People of God"—and that it should come *before* the chapter on the hierarchy.

The point the bishops at Vatican II wanted to make was clear: The whole people of God come before the hierarchy. What unites us is prior to what divides us. What we share in common thanks to our baptism and membership in the church is more important than the differences based on role or state of life.

The Constitution on the Church also describes the church as the *Body of Christ*. It borrows this image from Paul: just as a body has many parts (hands and arms, legs and feet), so too the church is made up of all kinds of people, with all kinds of gifts. Every member has a role to play. Every member is important. Even the parts of the body that seem less honorable are treated with even greater honor. All together these members contribute to the life and activity of the body. All are meant to work toward a single goal: to serve the life of the church and its mission in the world.

Finally, the church is the *temple of the Holy Spirit*. This image is biblical, just like the others. It calls to mind the charisms that we discussed at length in the previous chapter. It affirms that the incredible diversity of gifts that make up the church is divinely intended. It is the Spirit that grants these charisms. It is the Spirit that directs them toward service.

Vatican II had much, much more to say about the church. It lifted up the many vocations of the laity; it encouraged a more collegial exercise of authority; it invited internal church reform and renewal of church institutions; it called for reconciliation and dialogue among Christians; it spoke positively of the church's relationship to other religions; it fostered engagement with the broader world. But in the three biblical images described above we are reminded (1) that together we share a common identity and mission, (2) as a church made up of a diversity of roles, (3) empowered by gifts meant to serve the whole world.

Spiritual, But Not Religious

Can this hopeful vision of church be heard within a society that is becoming increasingly indifferent—even suspicious—toward organized religion?

Part of this suspicion comes from a broader cultural resistance to institutions in general. This is not new. Our American psyche has long been shaped by the principle of individual liberty and the myth of the "self-made man." We are skeptical of any institution or authority that tries to tell us what to do. Moreover, we know too well the failures of these institutions and those who represent them. Recent decades reveal one disappointment after another—Watergate, the Vietnam War, dishonest politicians, cheating athletes, failing schools, the collapse of big banks, government gridlock, and on and on. Even the church is not immune from such failure, as the tragedy of the sexual abuse scandal makes horrifically clear. People today have good reason to be skeptical of institutions, including religious institutions.

But there is another dynamic at work. More and more people are rejecting not only *religious institutions*, but also the very notion of *religious community*. It is not just the structures that people see as a problem, it is the whole idea that religion can be something more than an individual, private exercise. This view is captured by the well-worn phrase, "I am spiritual, but not religious." For many people, *spiritual* has a positive feel, evoking the desire for a personal relationship with God or some higher power, a more free-flowing sense of faith or purpose in life. *Religious* has a negative feel, evoking the rules and the rituals, the dogma and the dullness that go along with organized religion.

By claiming to be "spiritual, but not religious," many people today—particularly young people—are saying that they are hungry for meaning, but fed up with church. In fact, the fastest growing religious group in the United States are those who claim no affiliation with any religious group.

How should a church so deeply committed to the communal nature of faith respond to such developments? How should those of us in ministry respond?

We should begin by acknowledging that those rejecting "religion" in favor of "spirituality" are often expressing a legitimate concern and living out their own deep commitments. In their criticism of institutional hypocrisy and in their pursuit of a deeper spiritual life, they have a lot to teach us.

At the same time, we should also affirm that "the spiritual" can never be wholly separated from "the religious." The two need each other. Without spirituality, religion can become an empty shell of doctrines that fail to draw people into relationship with God. But without religion, spirituality can become self-centered and complacent, unable to challenge us when we veer off track. To acknowledge the importance of religion is to place one's personal relationship with God in the context of a larger religious community. And the real value of religious communities is that they keep us honest. They hold us accountable. They connect us to something bigger than ourselves and our own self-improvement. They call us to conversion.

Theology for Ministry

Given our contemporary cultural context, ministers today have a special responsibility to help their fellow believers see themselves as part of the church. Our faith is a communal faith, and discipleship entails living one's life as a member of the Body of Christ. This membership means that we recognize both what we receive from this community of faith and what we are called to give.

Unfortunately, many Catholics have little sense of themselves as active contributors to their religious tradition. This is particularly true among younger Catholics like the undergraduates I teach. They may admit that they have received a lot from their Catholic upbringing. But if they have any sense of *agency*—any sense of active participation—it is a sense of being agents of their personal *beliefs*, not agents of their *church*. They do not see themselves acting within their tradition, contributing to it, helping it to develop and grow. This should not surprise us. At church, young people are often socialized into passivity. Rarely have they been asked to help. Never have they felt authorized to act as leaders or representatives of their own religious tradition. The same could be said of many older Catholics as well.

The theologian Dennis Doyle draws a simple analogy. Think of Alcoholics Anonymous. A.A. is an extensive network of groups spread around the world. You can learn all about A.A. by visiting their website, reading articles online, or checking out books at the library. But probably the best way to learn about the organization is to talk to a member. Any member. Each and every member of A.A. sees himself or herself as a representative of the group. When someone needs help, A.A. members step up. They feel empowered to act on behalf of the organization.[6]

Wouldn't it be wonderful if every Catholic had the same sense of ownership and responsibility for the mission of the church? In its document on the liturgy, the Second Vatican Council warned that the laity should not come to Mass as "strangers or silent spectators" (*Sacrosanctum Concilium* 48). Instead all of the faithful are called to take a "full, conscious, and active part" in the celebration (*Sacrosanctum Concilium* 14). This call applies to all of church life. We are all called to full, conscious, and active participation in the life of the church.

Lay ministers have a special responsibility to foster this sense of ownership and participation among all of the laity. One of the most powerful ways lay ministers do so is by the way they model it through their own lives of service. Ministry is an *ecclesial* activity—it always takes place within and on behalf of the church community.

In ministry, there are no independent contractors. I may serve relatively free of bishops or priests, working outside the framework of a diocese or parish. Even so, I am part of a common project, working toward a common goal. Even if I serve alone, I still serve on behalf of the Body of Christ.

Here we have an invitation to see our own work in the context of a larger mission and purpose. It is the challenge to submit oneself both to the needs of the community and to the instruction of the community's leaders. It is the call to strive for communion with the church and its teaching.

But what if I disagree with what church leaders are saying or doing? What if I cannot accept a particular church teaching? Do I still serve as a minister *of the church*?

The Catholic tradition has long tried to uphold both the primacy of conscience, on the one hand, and the importance of a properly formed conscience, on the other. The first acknowledges that every human being can know right from wrong thanks to the law of God written in our hearts (CCC 1776). The second affirms that we also have the obligation to cultivate this interior sense by listening to the Word of God, the advice of others, and the authoritative teaching of the magisterium (the official teaching office of the church) (CCC 1785).

Thus we have an obligation to follow our conscience *and* an obligation to see that our conscience is formed by the teaching of the church. But what happens when we run into a conflict? What do we do when we find ourselves in a situation in which we know well what the magisterium teaches, but still cannot accept it? How do we know when we are being faithful and when we are being false?

That question can only be answered by God, who sees into our hearts more clearly than we can ever hope to see ourselves. But a few external signs accompany those who are acting faithfully, even when they disagree. First, the disagreement with church teaching is rare. It is not habitual or one's basic "default mode." Second, the disagreement comes after significant time spent in prayer, reflection, and conversation about the issue. Third, the individual who disagrees with the official teaching still recognizes the authority of the magisterium and its responsibility to teach on this particular topic. And finally, the decision to disagree comes with a feeling of sadness and pain, rather than pride or self-righteousness.

All of this demands a kind of humility on the part of the minister that is quite countercultural—particularly in a society that so values critical thinking and independence. As a minister, I am called not to abandon my own judgment, but to place it within a broader horizon—and to admit that there may be a wisdom that is wider than what I can see right now. Even if I end up disagreeing, the effort to struggle *with* the church's teaching is itself a sign of my commitment *to* it. Far worse than disagreement would be disinterest or disdain. To engage church teaching in thinking through difficult issues is to affirm that the church has something to say. It implies a commitment to work this out together.

An ecclesial approach to ministry includes both appreciation for all that we receive from the church and encouragement for all we have to contribute. Lay ministers model this kind of active engagement through active service within and on behalf of the church—a church that includes both clergy and laity, both institution and community, both visible realities and the invisible presence of God.

For Reflection and Discussion

1. Share what you saw when you meditated on the gospel passage at the start of this chapter. Name one of the friends or family members who carried you to Christ. What route did they take? What were the ways they brought you to faith?
2. What are the forces in society or the habits in your life that encourage individualism? Where have you found genuine community? Do you consider yourself more "spiritual" or more "religious"?
3. Describe your favorite church building. Why is it your favorite? Pretend that you have been asked to plan the basic design for a new church in your community. What would it look like and why?
4. If you were the bishop of your diocese, what would be your top three priorities? What concrete steps would you take to achieve them?

Recommended Reading

United States Catholic Catechism for Adults (Washington, DC: USCCB Publishing, 2006), chapter 10.

Catechism of the Catholic Church, second edition (Vatican City: Libreria Editrice Vaticana, 2000), nn. 748–870.

Gaillardetz, Richard R. *Ecclesiology for a Global Church: A People Called and Sent.* Maryknoll, NY: Orbis Books, 2008.

Hahnenberg, Edward P. *A Concise Guide to the Documents of Vatican II.* Cincinnati, OH: St. Anthony Messenger Press, 2007.

Harrington, Daniel J. *The Church According to the New Testament: What the Wisdom and Witness of Early Christianity Teach Us Today.* Chicago: Sheed & Ward, 2001.

McBrien, Richard P. *The Church: The Evolution of Catholicism.* New York: HarperCollins, 2008.

Second Vatican Council. Dogmatic Constitution on the Church (*Lumen Gentium*), http://www.vatican.va/archive/hist_councils/ii_vatican _council/documents/vat-ii_const_19641121_lumen-gentium_en .html.

6 For Others

Before the feast of Passover, Jesus knew that his hour had come to pass from this world to the Father. He loved his own in the world and he loved them to the end. The devil had already induced Judas, son of Simon the Iscariot, to hand him over. So, during supper, fully aware that the Father had put everything into his power and that he had come from God and was returning to God, he rose from supper and took off his outer garments. He took a towel and tied it around his waist. Then he poured water into a basin and began to wash the disciples' feet and dry them with the towel around his waist. (John 13:1-5)

Every Holy Thursday our parish reenacts this Last Supper scene. We watch as fellow parishioners process to the altar and take off their shoes and socks. We see our priest remove his vestments, crouch down, and pour water over their feet. Even in a big church, the ritual feels intimate. It evokes what those first disciples must have felt—Jesus is close, showing us something important.

Jesus became a servant to others. He literally acted like a slave, washing the feet of the dinner guests. He even washed the feet of Judas. Would that each of us could serve so selflessly. Would that each of us could live and act so radically *for others*.

After Jesus finished, he said to his disciples: "I have given you a model to follow, so that as I have done for you, you should also do" (John 13:15).

Starting with Experience

All of us have some experience serving others. When a friend needs us, we drop everything to help. When a neighbor asks, we lend a hand. Raising children is an incredible act of service. So is caring for aging parents. Part of being human is the call, at various times and in various ways, to serve.

Many of us also have experience serving others within or on behalf of the Christian community. We minister to the assembly by singing in the choir or distributing communion. We volunteer for the parish blood drive. We serve meals at the homeless shelter. We teach catechism. We give a *rollo* talk at a Cursillo retreat. We chaperone the youth group trip. We may even lead the youth group, or direct the religious education program, or coordinate the outreach programs for the parish.

All of these acts of service touch the lives of others.

Whose life have you touched? Whose feet have you washed?

Pause and reflect on your own experience. Think about the people you have served—either through formal ministry or more informal assistance. If it helps, call to mind one person. Close your eyes, image his or her face, and ask yourself: What was the need of this person? And how did I respond? What personal gifts did I bring to the encounter? What gifts did the other bring? As I ministered to this person, how did she or he minister to me? Craft a prayer in the form of a letter thanking this person for the way he or she helped you grow closer to God.

What is Ministry?

Ministry means "service." *Christian ministry* is service that flows from a relationship with Jesus and toward the reign of God that he proclaimed.

Here we turn our attention to a theology of Christian ministry. Everything we have covered in the chapters above—God's call in our lives, God's presence in our world, Jesus' preaching of the kingdom, the gifts of the Spirit, the nature of the church—all of this lays the foundation for a theology of ministry.

At the very start, it is helpful to distinguish Christian *ministry* from Christian *discipleship*. To be a disciple is literally to be a "learner" or a "listener." It is to follow the teacher, Jesus. Discipleship begins in baptism. It encompasses the whole of the Christian life. It takes place within the community called church. It entails nothing less than living out the reign of God—a life of loving relationship with God and with other people.

Ministry also flows out of baptism and membership in the church community. But it involves something more than living the Christian life. It involves taking up the mission of Jesus. It involves doing something to advance the kingdom of God. *Christian ministry is any activity, done on behalf of the church community, that proclaims, celebrates, and serves the reign of God.*

Ministry is not restricted to the activities of the ordained; nor is it equivalent to every good deed done by a Christian. Ministry involves a mission. It entails a relationship and a responsibility to the church community. It aims at the same goal that was the purpose of Jesus' life: to recognize and welcome the special presence of God in our midst.

Early Developments in Ministry

The New Testament reveals not only the impressive example of Jesus' own service, but also a variety of people drawn into his ministry. The Twelve Apostles are perhaps the most well-known of these early ministers. But the Apostle Paul, who was not one of the Twelve, interpreted his own vocation as a call to ministry. And he went on to call forth many others. Paul's letters list a host of coworkers (men and women) ministering alongside him: Timothy and Apollos, Phoebe and Epaphras, Tychichus and many others. The churches he served were marked by a dizzying diversity of charisms—gifts of the Spirit that Paul always tried to channel toward ministry.

Paul established churches in Corinth, Ephesus, and elsewhere. Then he moved on. Someone had to stay behind and see to the ongoing life of the community. Thus two kinds of ministry took shape during this early period: (1) ministry that flowed from the church's missionary enterprise (e.g., apostles, prophets, and teachers), and (2) ministry that involved the residential care of local communities (e.g., bishops, deacons, and presbyters).

We see a vivid illustration of these two types of ministry in the symbol of Peter. Peter was remembered as the great fisherman who became a "fisher of men" (Mark 1:17). This image fit nicely with the role of a missionary, who had to go out and "catch" others, bringing them into the community of faith. But by the end of John's gospel, a different image of Peter had emerged. John describes a conversation after the resurrection in which Jesus commanded Peter three times to "feed my sheep" (John 21:17). The fisherman had become a shepherd—an image that better symbolized the minister's role of caring for a flock already established.[1]

The concern for residential care led to the creation of three ministries that eventually became the three orders within the sacrament of holy orders: bishop, deacon, and presbyter. These ministries were originally borrowed from others. The role of presbyter (which today we call "priest") came from Jewish synagogues, which at the time often had a board of elders (*presbyteroi*) who oversaw the life of the community. The role of bishop and deacon came from the voluntary associations of Greek and Roman society. The officers of these "clubs" included overseers (*episkopoi*) and servants (*diakonoi*).

In adopting these roles from others, early Christians brought them together in a new way, creating a hybrid structure. By the second century, they had evolved into the classic Christian model of ministry: a bishop, surrounded by a group of presbyters and assisted by deacons and other ministers, served a local Christian community.

As the church grew, these leadership roles became increasingly formalized. The rise of a *clergy* (those "set apart" from the community) created a division between those who led and those who followed. The chasm between the two widened over the course of the Middle Ages. By the twelfth century, the influential canon lawyer Gratian would speak of two kinds of Christians: "the men of the church" (clergy) and "the men of the world" (laity). A dividing line had split the Body of Christ in two.

Clergy in the Church
Laity in the World

Dividing-Line Model of Ministry

In the centuries that followed, a variety of religious orders were founded. These cut across the dividing line in interesting ways, keeping alive a diversity of ministries. But in terms of the church's official theology, the ordained priesthood gradually absorbed all other ministries. Ministry came to mean status. It gave the priest a unique identity and exclusive power to administer the sacraments, to preach the word, and to lead the community.

In the middle of the twentieth century, a resurgence of lay activity challenged the dividing-line model of ministry. Church leaders wanted to encourage the laity, but they had a hard time imagining the laity with an active role in the church. So they described this "lay apostolate" as *a participation in the apostolate of the hierarchy*. In other words, the laity helped out with work that really belonged to the clergy. They had no proper ministry of their own.

The Rise of Lay Ministry

All of this changed with the Second Vatican Council. Vatican II taught that baptism incorporates the laity into the church, and thus into its saving mission. Thus the apostolate of the laity comes not from the hierarchy, but directly from Christ: "Through Baptism and Confirmation all are appointed to this apostolate by the Lord himself" (*Lumen Gentium* 33).

Inspired by this vision, a whole generation of Catholic laity entered into direct service within and on behalf of the church. The language of "lay apostolate" quickly gave way to "lay ministry" (According to Vatican II, "apostolate" is *any* participation in the mission of the church. Lay ministry is one form of this apostolate.)

In the United States, lay ministry appeared without much fanfare or fuss. There was no Vatican decree mandating these ministries. There was no national pastoral plan. Instead, these ministries emerged from the ground up. As Zeni Fox put it, the rise of lay ministry was a lot like Topsy: it "just growed."[2]

Following Vatican II, the church in the United States faced new needs. Reforms to the liturgy needed implementation and explanation. The revised Rite of Christian Initiation of Adults required sponsors and team leaders. Religious education moved beyond the parochial schools into a variety of parish programs. Emerging questions about civil rights, war, and poverty were recognized as concerns that churches needed to address. Adult Catholics sought opportunities to deepen their faith, to study the tradition, and to serve others.

In the midst of all these changes, people offered their help. Pastors began to hire their best volunteers, along with women religious seeking new forms of service, to bring some order to newly-created religious education programs in their parishes. The DRE was born!

The success of the Director of Religious Education model led to the creation of other roles on the parish staff. General assistants, called pastoral ministers or pastoral associates, appeared, as did youth ministers, liturgical coordinators, and directors of social concerns. The work of organists and other liturgical musicians was finally recognized as ministry.

At the same time, colleges and universities began to offer graduate courses and programs in theology for lay people.

Dioceses established offices for pastoral ministry. National and regional Encuentros encouraged participation and lay leadership. Pastoral centers opened. Professional organizations for lay ministers emerged.

Before Vatican II, parishes were led by a pastor and one or more associate pastors—with nuns in the school and a few lay people hired as organists or janitors. Now most parish offices house a team of lay ministers—directors of religious education, youth ministers, business managers, coordinators of liturgy, and directors of outreach.

Today there are more than 38,000 professionally-prepared lay ministers employed in U.S. parishes—more than the number of diocesan priests. And their numbers continue to grow. These lay leaders have come to be called *lay ecclesial ministers*. They are a standard feature of contemporary church life, and a welcome source of ministerial vitality. But they represent only a tiny fraction of the tens of thousands of lay women and men who serve in unpaid, occasional, but no less important, ministries. Lectors, eucharistic ministers, catechists, members of the parish council, movement leaders, translators, volunteers of all sorts—these lay ministers serve the church and the world in ways hard to imagine just fifty years ago.

In fact, if we step back and take the long view, we can honestly say that we have been living through one of the most significant periods of ministerial transformation in the history of the church.

Indeed, the rise of lay ministry stands out as one of the top three or four ministerial shifts of the past two thousand years. It is on a historical par with the changes to the church brought on by the rise of communal forms of monasticism in the fifth century, the birth of mendicant orders (e.g., Franciscans and Dominicans) in the thirteenth century, and the explosion of active women's religious communities in the nineteenth century.

These comparisons are not meant to suggest that lay ministry is a new type of religious order. But it is a new way of ministering, just as those new forms of religious life were in their day. We might miss the parallel if we get preoccupied with the vows of poverty, chastity, and obedience. Instead of looking through the lens of the *vows*, we ought to look through the lens of *ministry*—the concrete service that new religious orders offered the church. When that is our lens, then we begin to see the novelty, the originality, and the change that each new wave of religious life brought.[3]

Saints Francis and Dominic started something genuinely new: communities of men (and then women) who were not monks tied to a monastery, but friars free to preach in the streets of medieval cities. They sought university degrees, moved from diocese to diocese, and begged for a living—innovations meant for a new kind of ministry. Three hundred years later, the Jesuits would adapt, invigorate, or invent a host of new ministries— using books and sacred lectures, schools and spiritual direction, retreats and parish missions to "help souls." The active communities of women religious that exploded onto the scene in the eighteenth and nineteenth centuries shunned the cloister in order to serve the poor directly. Building hospitals, orphanages, and schools, they were ministerial trailblazers.

Each new wave of religious life brought a richness of ministry, a new way of being a minister, and an original form of serving the reign of God. The same is true with lay ministry today.

Two Conversations

All of these changes, however, do not mean that we have entirely escaped the legacy of the dividing-line model of ministry.

Several years ago I taught a course on ministry in a graduate program that included both seminarians and students preparing for lay ministry.

The class was a delight to teach. The students were bright and enthusiastic. They were deeply committed to Christ and to the church. They brought a variety of life experiences to the discussion. And they seemed to have a healthy mix of both idealism and realism about the future they faced as ministers.

The best part, though, was that everyone got along! These men and women had studied together for two years. They had formed friendships and had learned how to be honest and open with one another. I got the sense that they liked spending time together.

Yet, despite these almost ideal conditions for ministerial formation, there was still a kind of disconnect in the classroom between the seminarians and the lay ministry students.

There were no outright disagreements or big fights. The two groups just came to the class with different questions. And that meant they often had trouble hearing what the other group was trying to say.

On the one hand, the lay ministry students always seemed to be asking what it meant *to do ministry*. They were concerned about professional effectiveness. They wondered what roles they would play within a parish, school, hospital, or agency. They thought in terms of *function*.

On the other hand, the seminarians seemed mostly interested in what it meant *to be a minister*. They asked about the nature of ordained ministry. They were concerned about the status of priests and the meaning of priesthood. They thought in terms of *identity*.

These were two different conversations, and they went on in the same room for several weeks. The breakthrough moment of the course came when I simply brought this dynamic out into the open. By naming their differing concerns, each group could acknowledge its own perspective, along with the blind spots that went with it. We were then able to have a shared conversation.

What fascinated me about this experience was the way in which it almost perfectly reflected what I had been reading in the theological literature. Like our class, Catholic writing on ministry since Vatican II could almost be divided into two separate conversations.

One conversation revolves around priesthood. It tends to be very Christ-centered, in that it stresses the priest's ability to act "in the person of Christ" (*in persona Christi*) and represent Christ to the community. It emphasizes the "being" of the minister over the "doing" of the ministry, *identity* over function. Because this conversation describes ministry flowing down, through ordination, from Jesus to the apostles to the bishops to the priests, it could be called a theology "from above." This conversation goes on most often in seminaries, bishops' committees, and Vatican offices—the places most concerned with priestly formation.

A second conversation starts not with the ordained priest-hood, but with lay ministry. This conversation tends to be more Spirit-centered, in that it sees ministry inspired by the Spirit's charisms in the life of an individual. It emphasizes the "doing" of the ministry over the "being" of the minister, *function* over identity. Because it imagines ministry bubbling up from baptism, it could be called a theology "from below." This conversation takes place in universities, ministry formation programs, and national ministry associations.

These two conversations speak to different needs. Each is valuable in itself and makes an important contribution. The trouble is that the two rarely come together. But priests and lay ministers *do* come together in the day-to-day life of ministry! Thus the separation of theological conversations is worrisome. It has the potential to lead to different expectations, miscom-munication, and misunderstanding. What we need is a common language. We need a way to bring together Christ-centered and Spirit-centered conversations about ministry.

The best way to do so, it seems to me, is to turn to the Trinity.

A Trinitarian Theology of Ministry

For Christians, the Trinity represents the perfect example of unity in diversity. Christ and Spirit cannot be separated. To-gether with the Father, they constitute the one God who is the source and goal of every ministry.

As we saw in chapter 2, the doctrine of the Trinity not only affirms a God who is three-in-one, it also affirms a God who is fundamentally relational. God is not an isolated individual or a lonely king. God is a dynamic communion of love—Father, Son, and Holy Spirit—who spills over in order to draw us all into the divine life.

A trinitarian approach to ministry is a relational approach to ministry. Ministers are not isolated individuals whose relationships are secondary to their existence as ministers. In fact, one becomes a minister precisely by entering into and being established in relationships of service. Like the three persons of the Trinity, ministers find their identity and purpose in relationship.

It's not just that priests and lay ministers are involved in two separate conversations, it's that they are speaking two different languages! One uses words like "being" and "identity." The other uses words like "doing" and "function." A relational approach opens a third way, offering the possibility of a shared vocabulary. It breaks us out of the stalemate by pushing beyond identity and function to *relationship*. Our ministry cannot be reduced to who we are or what we do. It includes both of these and something more—our relationships with God, the church community, and the people we serve.

These ministerial relationships exist, first of all, at the interpersonal level. *Interpersonal relationships* are what we usually think of when we hear the word "relationship." This is the level of basic human contact. The conversation between a hospital chaplain and a grieving parent. The friendship between a director of religious education and a volunteer catechist. The fellowship that forms among *cursillistas*. The respect and trust between a bishop and a pastoral coordinator. Gestures of care, offers of help, moments or months of presence to an individual in need. This is the heart of ministry, people touching the lives of other people, and being touched by them.

When interpersonal relationships take on a public dimension, when they involve ministry done on behalf of the church, and are formally integrated into the church's mission, then they become *ecclesial relationships*. The liturgy coordinator functions as part of a parish staff. The catechist serves on a team. The campus minister reports to school officials and organizes programs in cooperation with local churches. On moving to a new parish, a pastor does not necessarily become every parishioner's friend. That is the level of the interpersonal. However, he does become a ministerial representative with responsibility for leadership and coordination on behalf of every parishioner within the community. He enters into an ecclesial relationship.

Consider the following example. A concerned friend who visits a fellow parishioner in the hospital may be motivated to do so not only by friendship but also by her Christian conviction that this is what Jesus would do. Such an act may transform the parishioners' interpersonal relationship, but it does not significantly alter either person's ecclesial relationships. The friend is simply fulfilling her baptismal call. She is affirming her place as an active member of the church community.

However, if another parishioner visits a sick individual or an elderly shut-in as part of a parish program or as a member of a visitation team, the visitor's ecclesial relationships are transformed. She takes on a new position on behalf of the larger church. A combination of the parishioner's decision, the public nature of the ministry, and the designation or recognition of her ministry by the church community and its leadership contributes to her new place among the various ministerial relationships that make up the church.[4]

Beyond the Dividing Line

A relational approach to ministry moves us beyond a model based on a dividing line between clergy and laity. The problem with the clergy–laity distinction is not that it is wrong. The problem is that it is too blunt of an edge to mark out the diversity of ministerial relationships that make up the church today.

Vatican II did not eliminate the distinction between clergy and laity, but it did move beyond a simplistic separation between "clergy in the church" and "laity in the world." It did so in at least two ways.

First, Vatican II insisted that *we are all the church*. The idea that the laity interact with "the church" as if it were a separate entity makes little sense in light of the council's teaching that the laity and clergy together constitute the one people of God. The laity are not outside of or apart from the church. We are all the church.

Second, Vatican II taught that *the whole church is in the world.* As we saw in chapter 1, the council described life in the secular world as the special characteristic of the laity (*Lumen Gentium* 31). But that description needs to be placed within the broader context of the council's affirmation that the *whole church* lives within and seeks to transform the world. The whole church, both "'a visible organization and a spiritual community,' travels the same journey as all of humanity and shares the same earthly lot with the world: is to be a leaven and, as it were, the soul of human society in its renewal by Christ and transformation into the family of God" (*Gaudium et Spes* 40). Thus "the world" is not the exclusive concern of the laity, it includes every single member of the Body of Christ.

Thus the dividing line gives way to a model of concentric circles in which the many ministers that serve the mission of Christ fall within the church, which as a whole falls within the world of God's creation.

Many Ministries

Within the world is the church. And within the church are a diversity of ministries that serve its life and mission. The great

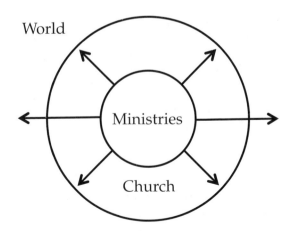

Concentric-Circles Model of Ministry

gain of a trinitarian theology of ministry is that it shows us how different ministries follow on a diversity of ecclesial relationships—just as the different persons of the Trinity flow out of the relationships that constitute the one God.

The ecclesial relationships of the minister are shaped by three things: (1) the level of vocational commitment on the part of the minister, (2) the type of ministry involved, and (3) the recognition that comes from the church community and its leadership. These determine the "place" or "position" of a ministry within the church. In other words, different ministries have different positions thanks to their differing ecclesial relationships.

The ordained ministries of bishop, priest, and deacon represent three different sets of these ecclesial relationships.

The *bishop* is first and foremost a minister of communion. He has the responsibility to serve and strengthen the relationships (the communion) that exist (1) within the local church that we call the diocese, (2) among the many local churches that constitute the one, universal church, and (3) between the church of our own time and the church of the apostles.

The *priest* makes the bishop present within the parish, keeping this particular community in communion with the larger church. He presides over the Eucharist because he presides over the community. And his priesthood takes on meaning only within and in relation to the larger reality of the priesthood of all the faithful. As the *Catechism of the Catholic Church* explains, "the ministerial priesthood is at the service of the common priesthood. It is directed at the unfolding of the baptismal grace of all Christians" (CCC 1547).

The *deacon* is ordained "not for the priesthood, but for the ministry" (*Lumen Gentium* 29). Although he usually serves alongside the priest and lay ministers within a parish, the deacon enjoys a special relationship to the bishop—who sends the deacon into relationship with others, particularly those on the margins, through ministries of service, compassion, charity, and justice.

Members of *religious orders* embrace life in community and the vows of poverty, chastity, and obedience. This way of life (known as "the consecrated life") arose in the church among individuals and groups seeking total dedication to Christ and an imitation of his life. Their relationship to the broader church came primarily through their radical witness. But as we saw above, this way of life quickly opened out into a diversity of ministerial relationships. Religious women, in particular, came to occupy a distinctive ecclesial position. Publically recognized and present within local communities, they ministered in relationship to, but with a certain independence from, the hierarchy. Their way of life made possible new ecclesial relationships and new forms of ministry.

Different lay ministries also entail different ecclesial relationships. Several years ago, the U.S. Bishops drew attention to this diversity by distinguishing *lay ecclesial ministry* from lay ministry more broadly understood. Their document *Co-Workers in the Vineyard of the Lord* focused on these lay women and men who serve more-or-less full time, more-or-less long term, in positions of ministerial leadership. Lay ecclesial ministers are the directors of religious education, the youth ministers, the liturgical coordinators, the pastoral associates, and the social justice ministers who have become so much a part of our parish experience. *Co-Workers* lists four characteristics that distinguish this group from other lay ministers: (1) authorization to serve publicly in the local church, (2) leadership in an area of ministry, (3) close mutual collaboration with the ordained, and (4) preparation appropriate to their level of responsibility.[5] Given their roles of leadership and coordination, these lay ecclesial ministers are not just ministers in relationship with others, they are ministers with a special responsibility for *fostering* ministerial relationships among others.

Beyond this group of professional lay leaders is the reality of *lay ministers* who serve in more occasional ways, usually in a volunteer capacity or in response to a particular need. These ministers far outnumber lay ecclesial ministers and their service is essential to the life of the church. Lectors, eucharistic ministers, catechists, those who lead small faith-sharing groups or movements, regular volunteers at the homeless shelter, the retired accountant who coordinates hospital visits for the parish, the mom who sits on the pastoral council, the teens who rake the yards of shut-ins—all of these ministers engage in service done on behalf of the community. Their ministry flows out of relationship and into relationship.

These broad categories give just a glimpse into the diversity of ministries today. Since the call to ministry extends to all the baptized, many more particular examples could be added. We could include the growing phenomenon of religious associates— lay women and men who attach themselves to the charism of a particular religious community, serving out of that distinctive spirituality. We could add the many young Catholics who commit to a year or more of service before moving into a career, or the lay leaders working within Catholic hospitals and universities, who are being called to carry forward the mission of these institutions with a new sense of intentionality. Ecclesial movements like RENEW or the Catholic Charismatic Renewal are a source and a support for multiple ministries both within the parish and beyond its boundaries.

A fuller elaboration of all of these forms of ministry would paint in ever more vivid colors the variety of relationships that constitute the church. The thing that holds them all together is that which these ministries serve: the mission of Christ.

One Mission

Ministry is important, but only because it serves a larger mission.

Jesus saw himself on a mission. It was a mission centered on the reign of God. "To the other towns also I must proclaim the good news of the kingdom of God, because for this purpose I have been sent" (Luke 4:43). This kingdom was neither a political power nor a spiritual symbol. It was (and is) the special presence of God alive in the world—an offer of friendship that frees us from our selfishness and sin, letting us loose into a new and fuller life.

The kingdom of God is *euangelion—good news*. Jesus' mission was one of evangelization—spreading the good news of God's love for us. Our own ministries, whatever they may be, all share in this one mission of evangelization.

The word "evangelization" is rare among lay Catholics. For many, it sounds too Protestant or too preachy. It conjures up the image of a televangelist or a megachurch. We Catholics pray, we go to church, we serve others, we even minister. But we do not *evangelize*. (There's an old joke that asks: What do you get when you cross a Jehovah's Witness with a Catholic? Somebody who rings the doorbell and then has nothing to say!)

Gladly, some of this has started to change, at least at official levels. Embracing a broader notion of evangelization as synonymous with the mission of the church, Catholic leaders in recent decades have reclaimed this biblical language.

Pope Paul VI began this recovery with his 1975 document, Evangelization in the Modern World (*Evangelii Nuntiandi*), in which he described evangelization as the essential mission of the church. Pope John Paul II called for a "New Evangelization," and made this phrase a hallmark of his papacy. Pope Benedict XVI carried this emphasis forward, establishing a Pontifical Council for Promoting the New Evangelization and dedicating the 2012 synod of bishops to the theme. In his own later reflections on this synod, Pope Francis called the whole church to take part in this new missionary "going forth"—to leave behind "our own comfort zone in order to reach all the 'peripheries' in need of the light of the Gospel."[6]

What makes the New Evangelization "new" is not the message—the good news of God's reign remains the same. Rather, it is new in approach, attitude, and scope. It is an evangelization directed not to an unknown unbeliever in an unfamiliar corner of the world. Instead it is an evangelization directed to the whole world, its many cultures and its peoples, both those who have never heard of Christ and those who have heard the good news but forgotten what it means to follow Jesus.

The New Evangelization includes not only initial proclamation, but also pastoral care, concrete service, and the re-evangelization of those whose lives are no longer inspired by the Gospel. Alongside preaching, the New Evangelization demands dialogue. It requires serious attention to full human development—including freedom from poverty, violence, and unjust structures of oppression. The New Evangelization employs the best of modern media, while respecting the dignity and conscience of those who listen and respond. And it calls everyone in the church to participate in Jesus' original mission of spreading the joy, peace, and purpose of the kingdom of God. As we saw in chapter 3, the mission of Jesus involved more than just words. When the disciples of John the Baptist came to him to ask if he were the Messiah, Jesus replied, "Go and tell John what you hear and see: the blind regain their sight, the lame walk, lepers are cleansed, the deaf hear, the dead are raised, and the poor have the good news proclaimed to them" (Matt 11:4-5).

Ministry today finds its inspiration in the evangelizing mission of Jesus. It begins in baptism, takes shape in words and deeds, and points toward the reign of God.

Theology for Ministry

Following the trinitarian, relational approach developed in this chapter, we can say that evangelization today is as much about connecting with others as it is about communicating. It is as much about *presence* as it is about *proclamation.*

The ministry of Jesus involved words, and they were important. But these words were lived out in actions. They took place in relationship. Jesus did not remain at a distance. His mission drew him close. If the church's ministry flows out of the trinitarian missions of Christ and the Spirit, then our ministry ought to reflect God's great desire to be close to humanity. It ought to reflect something of the humility of Jesus,

> Who, though he was in the form of God,
>> did not regard equality with God something to be grasped.
>> Rather, he emptied himself,
>> taking the form of a slave,
>> coming in human likeness. (Phil 2:6-7)

The communion of the Trinity is not closed in on itself. It reaches out. It extends in mission. It enters into relationship. The God who is *for us* is the God who wants to be *with us*.

Earlier we took up Jesus' parable of the Good Samaritan. The story begins with a question. A scribe asks Jesus, "And who is my neighbor?" The story ends not with an answer, but with another, slightly different, question. After describing the actions of the priest, the Levite, and the Samaritan, Jesus now asks the scribe, "Which of these three was a neighbor?"

Rather than tell us who our neighbor is, Jesus challenges us *to be* a neighbor.

To be a neighbor is to be the Samaritan. It is to cross over to the other side of the road and enter into the life of another. Years ago the Peruvian theologian Gustavo Gutiérrez made precisely this point.[7] He used the parable of the Good Samaritan to argue that ministry demands *solidarity* with those we serve. We must *become a neighbor* to others so that we can begin to hear their concerns, feel their needs, and see the world from their point of view. Like the Samaritan, we must *cross over* to the abused and neglected one on the side of the road. Where we stand determines what we will see.

Gutiérrez's first concern was that we see the poor of the world—particularly the poor of his native Latin America—the scandalous tragedy of millions of people "left on the side of the road." Following in this same spirit, Pope Francis has expanded the concern, speaking of the need for the church to go out to those on all the peripheries of life—those on the edge of sin, pain, injustice, ignorance, indifference to religion, and all forms of misery. As individual Christians and as a church, we must become present to those on the margins.

In our diverse and deeply-divided world, ministry demands a good deal of listening. We have so much to learn from those who suffer. We have so much to gain by attending to those who are overlooked or ignored. Those at the very beginning and those at the very end of life, those on the periphery of pain, those on the edge of belief, those on the boundaries of what we find acceptable—all are children of God, and all have something to teach us. Even those who are critics of the church see things that we need to recognize. Even those who deny God speak a language we need to understand.

People who enter ministry are so often filled with the fire of faith. There is so much we want to do. There is so much we want to say. We need to hang onto that passion and that joy. But a spirituality of loving presence calls us to a mutuality in ministry. It invites us into an openness captured beautifully in Richard Gillard's hymn, "The Servant Song":

> Will you let me be your servant,
>   let me be as Christ to you?
> Pray that I may have the grace
>   to let you be my servant too.

Solidarity, presence, mutuality—these are the marks of a ministerial spirituality marked by mission understood in terms of relationship. We do not so much act on others as accompany them. We give and we receive. We share together the good news of God's presence in the world.

None of these remarks should dismiss legitimate concerns about professional boundaries, appropriate self-care, or the need to know when a referral is necessary. The call to enter into the lives of those we serve is not an excuse to abandon our faith commitments, training, or common sense. Rather, a spirituality of presence is meant to suggest a basic stance—an attitude of empathy and compassion—that frees us to recognize how God is already at work in those we are called to serve.

For Reflection and Discussion

1. Share the thank you letter you wrote at the beginning of the chapter. How have you been ministered to by those you serve? Give one concrete example.
2. Not every good deed done by a Christian is ministry. Do you agree? What, in your mind, are the essential components of ministry?

3. List all the ministers (ordained, laity on staff, volunteers, etc.)
   active in your parish. How do they fit within the model suggested above? Describe their differing ecclesial relationships
   based on their differing levels of vocational commitment,
   type of ministry, and official recognition. Which of these three
   elements do you see as most important in determining the
   "place" of the minister in the community?
4. How well does your community reach out to those on "the
   peripheries of life"? What more needs to be done?

Recommended Reading

United States Catholic Catechism for Adults (Washington, DC: USCCB
   Publishing, 2006), chapter 11.
Catechism of the Catholic Church, second edition (Vatican City: Libreria
   Editrice Vaticana, 2000), nn. 871–975.

Cahoy, William J., ed. *In the Name of the Church: Vocation and Authoriza-
   tion of Lay Ecclesial Ministry.* Collegeville, MN: Liturgical Press,
   2012.
Eschenauer, Donna M., and Harold Daly Horell, eds. *Reflections on
   Renewal: Lay Ecclesial Ministry and the Church.* Collegeville, MN:
   Liturgical Press, 2011.
Fox, Zeni, ed. *Lay Ecclesial Ministry: Pathways Toward the Future.* Lanham,
   MD: Sheed & Ward, 2010.
Hahnenberg, Edward P. *Ministries: A Relational Approach.* New York:
   Crossroad Publishing, 2003.
U.S. Conference of Catholic Bishops. *Co-Workers in the Vineyard of the
   Lord: A Resource for Guiding the Development of Lay Ecclesial Ministry.*
   Washington, DC: USCCB Publishing, 2005.
Wood, Susan K., ed. *Ordering the Baptismal Priesthood: Theologies of Lay
   and Ordained Ministry.* Collegeville, MN: Liturgical Press, 2003.

Appendix

Theological Reflection in Group Settings

One tool used in ministry formation programs is Group Theological Reflection. The process provides a structured way to help people make connections between their faith tradition and their life experiences. In the context of a class or a small Christian community, members take turns sharing a personal story (using a narrative written in advance). The rest of the group then helps to "unpack" the theological significance of the event. One model for this process includes the following steps:[1]

1. *Select an Experience*. When it is your turn to present, choose one recent event (a "slice" of your experience) that raised for you important personal, theological, or ministerial questions. This event need not be dramatic or life-altering. Seemingly ordinary encounters or situations can offer much food for thought. However, the experience should contain some complexity or tension. Something about it should have challenged you or got you thinking.

2. *Prepare a Written Narrative*. Spend some time thinking about this experience, reviewing it in your mind, reflecting on what happened and how you felt. Then write a one-page, single-spaced summary of the event. The narrative should include brief background and a concise description of both what

happened (facts) and how you felt during the experience (feelings). This report is simply a straightforward description of the facts and your feelings. You should not get into defending your actions, guessing others' motives, or jumping ahead to assign meaning to the events.

3. *Group Discussion.* The Group Theological Reflection begins with the presenter reading the prepared narrative. (It is helpful if everyone has a copy.) A good facilitator can then move the conversation through two stages.

   The first stage is an initial response to the narrative. This is the time for group members to ask clarification questions, to name the parts of the story that struck them or engaged them, to share initial reactions, and to identify feelings and images from their own experience that were evoked by the story. The point is not to offer advice, but to try to identify or sympathize with some aspect of the experience. The presenter does not need to defend her or his actions, nor answer every question.

   The second stage is the properly theological component. Here the group draws on the language, images, and stories from our faith tradition to see how these might illuminate this experience. There are various sources that can be tapped: scripture, history, doctrine, morality, worship—even the ideas in this book! But it is important to keep in mind that the conversation is not meant to be a therapy session or an exercise in problem-solving. Rather, the group takes an experience and holds it alongside the themes of our faith, in order to see what insight might emerge. Through this process, the members of the group begin to learn how to relate their faith tradition to their day-to-day lives. Given the nature of such a conversation and the trust it requires, the expectation is that it remain confidential. What is said in the group stays in the group.

4. *Lived Response.* In the context of group reflection, the presenter may ask what she or he will do next. But it is only afterwards that the individual begins to apply his or her newfound insight in the context of life.

Notes

Preface, pages ix–xiii

1. Kenneth R. Overberg, *Roots & Branches: Grounding Religion in Human Experience*, rev. ed. (Kansas City, MO: Sheed & Ward, 1991), 135.

Chapter 1, pages 1–22

1. References to the documents of Vatican II are given by section number, not by page. The translation cited is Austin Flannery, ed., *Vatican Council II: The Basic Sixteen Documents* (Northport, NY: Costello Publishing, 1996).

2. Donald Senior, "Answering the Call: Biblical Perspectives," in *Catholics on Call: Discerning a Life of Service in the Church*, ed. Robin Ryan (Collegeville, MN: Liturgical Press, 2010), 16–17.

3. U.S. Conference of Catholic Bishops, *United States Catholic Catechism for Adults* (Washington, DC: USCCB Publishing, 2006), 531.

4. Marie Theresa Coombs and Francis Kelly Nemeck, *Called By God: A Theology of Vocation and Lifelong Commitment* (Collegeville, MN: Liturgical Press, 1992), 1–4.

5. Thomas Merton, *Seeds of Contemplation* (Norfolk, CT: New Directions, 1949), 26.

6. John Paul II, *The Consecrated Life (Vita Consecrata)* (Washington, DC: United States Catholic Conference, 1996), n. 31.

7. U.S. Conference of Catholic Bishops, *Co-Workers in the Vineyard of the Lord: A Resource for Guiding the Development of Lay Ecclesial Ministry* (Washington, DC: USCCB Publishing, 2005), 8.

8. Subcommittee on Lay Ministry, *Lay Ecclesial Ministry: The State of the Questions* (Washington, DC: United States Catholic Conference, 1999), 27.

9. *Co-Workers in the Vineyard*, 29.

Chapter 2, pages 23–44

1. Anne Tyler, *Dinner at the Homesick Restaurant* (New York: Alfred A. Knopf, 1982), 277.

2. Thomas F. O'Meara, *A Theologian's Journey* (Mahwah, NJ: Paulist Press, 2002), 16.

3. Michael J. Himes, *Doing the Truth in Love: Conversations about God, Relationships, and Service* (Mahwah, NJ: Paulist Press, 1995), 12.

4. *Summa Theologiae* I.3.4, in Thomas Aquinas, *Summa Theologiae*, vol. 2, trans. Timothy McDermott (New York: McGraw-Hill, 1964), 31–35.

5. *United States Catholic Catechism for Adults*, 53.

6. *Summa Theologiae* I.29.4, in Thomas Aquinas, *Summa Theologiae*, vol. 6, trans. Ceslaus Velecky (New York: McGraw-Hill, 1965), 61.

7. References to the *Catechism of the Catholic Church* are given by article number, not by page. The edition used here is *Catechism of the Catholic Church: Modifications from the* Editio Typica (New York: Doubleday, 1997).

8. *Howard Thurman: Essential Writings*, selected with an introduction by Luther E. Smith (Maryknoll, NY: Orbis Books, 2006), 41.

9. Cited in Elizabeth A. Johnson, *She Who Is: The Mystery of God in Feminist Theological Discourse* (New York: Crosssroad, 1992), 172.

10. Richard R. Gaillardetz, *A Vision of Pastoral Ministry* (Liguori, MO: Liguori, 2002), 13–16.

11. Ibid., 29–38.

Chapter 3, pages 45–66

1. Donald Senior, *Jesus: A Gospel Portrait* (Mahwah, NJ: Paulist Press, 1992), 7-10.

2. William P. Loewe, *The College Student's Introduction to Christology* (Collegeville, MN: Liturgical Press), 57.

3. Karl Rahner, *Foundations of Christian Faith: An Introduction to the Idea of Christianity* (New York: Crossroad, 1978), 226.

Chapter 4, pages 67–85

1. Johnson, *She Who Is*, 127.

2. Cited in *United States Catholic Catechism for Adults*, 104.

3. Johnson, *She Who Is*, 122–23.

4. *Summa Theologiae* I.28.2, in Thomas Aquinas, *Summa Theologiae*, vol. 7, trans. T. C. O'Brien (New York: McGraw-Hill, 1976), 95.

5. Quoted in Robert Coles, *The Call of Service: A Witness to Idealism* (New York: Houghton Mifflin, 1993), 3.

6. Robert Barron, *Catholicism: A Journey to the Heart of the Faith* (New York: Image Books, 2011), 197.

7. C. S. Lewis, *Mere Christianity* (New York: Macmillan, 1952), 190.

8. Leo Josef Suenens, "The Charismatic Dimension of the Church," in *Council Speeches of Vatican II*, ed. Hans Küng, Yves Congar, and Daniel O'Hanlon (Glen Rock, NJ: Paulist Press, 1964), 32–33.

9. John C. Haughey, "Charisms: An Ecclesiological Exploration," in *Retrieving Charisms for the Twenty-First Century*, ed. Doris Donnelly (Collegeville, MN: Liturgical Press, 1999), 1.

10. Ibid., 2.

11. Ibid., 2.

12. Ibid., 3.

13. Frederick Buechner, *Wishful Thinking: A Theological ABC* (New York: Harper & Row, 1973), 95.

14. Karl Barth, *Church Dogmatics*, Vol. III/4, *The Doctrine of Creation,* translated by A.T. Mackay (Edinburgh: T. & T. Clark, 1961), 569.

15. "Archbishop Oscar Romero Prayer: A Step Along the Way," http://www.usccb.org/prayer-and-worship/prayers/archbishop_romero_prayer.cfm.

16. Himes, *Doing the Truth in Love*, 59.

17. Parker J. Palmer, *Let Your Life Speak: Listening for the Voice of Vocation* (San Francisco: Jossey-Bass, 2000), 49.

Chapter 5, pages 86–106

1. Andrew M. Greeley, "It's Fun to Be Catholic," in *I Like Being Catholic: Treasured Traditions, Rituals, and Stories*, ed. Michael Leach and Therese J. Borchard (New York: Doubleday, 2000), 6.

2. John Paul II, *I Will Give You Shepherds: On the Formation of Priests in the Circumstances of the Present Day (Pastores Dabo Vobis)* (Washington, DC: United States Catholic Conference, 1992), n. 35.

3. Rodney Stark, *The Rise of Christianity: How the Obscure, Marginal Jesus Movement Became the Dominant Religious Force in the Western World in a Few Centuries* (San Francisco: HarperCollins, 1997), 7.

4. Daniel J. Harrington, *The Church According to the New Testament: What the Wisdom and Witness of Early Christianity Teach Us Today* (Chicago: Sheed & Ward, 2001), 112.

5. The following presentation was inspired by Thomas F. O'Meara, *Theology of Ministry*, rev. ed. (Mahwah, NJ: Paulist Press, 1999), 80-138.

6. Dennis M. Doyle, *The Church Emerging from Vatican II: A Popular Approach to Contemporary Catholicism*, rev. ed. (Mystic, CT: Twenty-Third Publications, 2002), 114.

Chapter 6, pages 107–27

1. Raymond E. Brown, *The Churches the Apostles Left Behind* (Mahwah, NJ: Paulist Press, 1984), 32.

2. Zeni Fox, *New Ecclesial Ministry: Lay Professionals Serving the Church*, rev. ed. (Chicago: Sheed & Ward, 2002), 4.

3. John W. O'Malley, "Priesthood, Ministry, and Religious Life: Some Historical and Historiographical Considerations," *Theological Studies* 49 (1988): 223-57.

4. Richard R. Gaillardetz, "Shifting Meanings in the Lay-Clergy Distinction," *Irish Theological Quarterly* 64 (1999): 135.

5. *Co-Workers in the Vineyard*, 10.

6. Pope Francis, *The Joy of the Gospel: On the Proclamation of the Gospel in Today's World (Evangelii Gaudium)* (Washington, DC: USCCB Publishing, 2013), n. 20.

7. Gustavo Gutiérrez, "Toward a Theology of Liberation," in *Liberation Theology: A Documentary History*, ed. Alfred T. Hennelly (Maryknoll, NY: Orbis Books, 1990), 62–76.

Appendix, pages 128–29

1. For a fuller, but very accessible, introduction to this process, see Robert L. Kinast, *Making Faith-Sense: Theological Reflection in Everyday Life* (Collegeville, MN: Liturgical Press, 1999).